SO FAR, SO GOOD

So Far, So Good

The First 94 Years

Roy R. Neuberger

with Alfred & Roma Connable

John Wiley & Sons, Inc.

New York • Chichester • Weinheim • Brisbane • Singapore • Toronto

Library of Congress Cataloging in Publication Data:
Neuberger, Roy R.
     So far, so good : the first 94 years / Roy R.
Neuberger.
          p.   cm.
     Includes index.
     ISBN 0-471-17186-7 (cloth : alk. paper)
     1. Neuberger, Roy R.   2. Capitalists and financiers—Biography.
3. Investments.   I. Title.
HG172.N48A3   1997
332.6'092—dc21
[B]   97-14193

Printed in the United States of America

10 9 8 7 6 5 4 3 2 1

This book is dedicated with love to my large and unique family—one wife, three children, eight grandchildren, seven great-grandchildren and counting. So far, so good.

Foreword

Several decades ago, I was working on my first television project—a prime-time network special about Wall Street. We shot the tense, ticking seconds of the bidding on a bond issue. We followed an early, hot, Fidelity manager, Gerry Tsai, as he set up his own fund. And then we found something unexpected—an exuberant Wall Street executive who clearly loved his work, but whose passion was something else: art. "I discovered art in the twenties," Roy Neuberger told us, "and I knew I wanted to collect it. I thought it was unfair that talented artists should starve, that Van Gogh could not sell a painting. I wanted to buy the work of living artists. But where was I to get the money? I asked myself, 'Where is there money?' The answer was Wall Street."

The director of that show couldn't get enough of Roy Neuberger. He said the camera loved him. It was Roy's interview that gave us the title: "Wall Street: Where the Money Is." Roll those black-and-white images today, and you are charmed by this fellow who will talk to you about finance but really wants to show you his paintings. Roy certainly did find where the money is. He enjoyed getting it, spending it, and giving it away as art. His legacy can be seen in the sensibility at the Neuberger Museum and in his other collections.

Roy is still working, at 94. When he was born in 1903, as he says, Teddy Roosevelt was president, the Wright brothers had yet to fly, and horses brought his father home from work. That gives you some perspective. Roy was in Paris in the twenties, with its lively art scene. He came to Wall Street in time to sample the headiness of that bull market frenzy and to be a first-hand witness to the 1929 crash. He survived it because, although he owned some stocks, he had sold Radio (RCA) short. Radio was the great fad stock of the day, and he made on its decline what he lost on the rest. It gave him a taste for hedging, and he still does it today, as an anchor to windward. (Warren Buffett, take note: today he is short Coca-Cola, one of your favorite stocks, as an anchor to windward.) Roy became a pioneer in the mutual fund industry. He isn't shy about coming up with ten rules for successful investing, either. He calls the market of the 1990s neither bull nor bear but the Sheep Market, after the behavior of some of its participants, and he will tell you why the "10 percent rule" will save you money.

Roy converted the rewards of his Wall Street talents into canvas. He met some of the outstanding artists of his day and built a noteworthy art collection. When Nelson Rockefeller was governor of New York, he was a formidable figure. He would greet you with a big grin, seize you by the hand and elbow, and tell you why you ought to do what he wanted. What he wanted from Roy, he said, at lunch at his estate, was his art collection. "Give us that collection," Rockefeller said, "and I will build you a museum." (In this case, "I" meant the State of New York, more precisely the State University of New York at Purchase. Rockefeller frequently confused the pronoun "I" and the State.) Parting with a collection that has been built by climbing stairs to the studios of artists cannot have been an easy decision, and Roy didn't accept Rockefeller's offer on the spot. But he did donate the collection, and Rockefeller—or New York State—did build the museum; so now the public can share the experience.

Roy never graduated from college, much less from business school. How, then, did he succeed? "I am convinced," he says, "that my success came from a curiosity about life. Trading securities requires a lot of intuition, something you can only develop as a student of life. In Paris, and ever since, I have been studying constantly. I study people, I study life, I look and listen and read. I never found learning about anything a waste of time."

Recently, Roy was a guest of honor at the annual dinner of an association of gerontologists—people who study how and why we age. Here was a man who was 93 years old, still working, and still enjoying himself. One of the scientists had already asked Roy if, in the interests of the study, he would mind being poked and prodded a bit and if he would donate a blood sample. Roy was called to the microphone to say a few words about successful aging. At my table, the association's past president took out a pen and a pocket notebook as Roy started.

Roy said exercise was important. In his youth he had played a lot of competitive tennis, and even today, he worked out with a personal trainer three times a week and made a point of walking in the park. The scientists all nodded wisely. "I am still interested in the stock market," he continued. "When you are 93, I have to tell you, tennis fades, and so does sex, but there's still the market." That really warmed up the audience.

But most important, Roy said: "I still have my curiosity. I want to know why things happen. So I still greet each day with enthusiasm because I want to see what will happen next, and I know I will learn something new."

And that brought the crowd to its feet.

ADAM SMITH

Preface

Some people waste their lives in the constant pursuit of great wealth. As a commodity, let's face it, money doesn't rate as high as good health—and it certainly isn't up there with great art.

Money in and of itself has never really interested me. The driving passions of my career and my life have been the art of trading and the support of art. Money, of course, has been the by-product of trading that enabled me to purchase great art and support culture.

When I arrived on Wall Street in 1929, one of my first jobs was managing a small portfolio of my own money. Soon after that, I embarked on a career of managing other people's portfolios as well. In only a few years, I had exceeded my wildest dreams. Today my brokerage house, Neuberger&Berman, manages about $50 billion.

Wall Street has been wonderful to me. I arrived there just before the Stock Market Panic of 1929—and did well. What I learned in 1929 helped me immensely when the stock market collapsed again in 1987. And it has prepared me for the erratic markets of the 1990s. I may well be the only person still active on Wall Street who was working there at the time of both panics— 1929 and 1987—and didn't blink either time.

My timing has always been lucky—I was an American in Paris during the great cultural explosion in the mid-1920s. And I was an avid reader. When I discovered the wonderful biography *Vincent Van Gogh* by Floret Fels, I learned that Van Gogh had sold only one painting during his lifetime. He died alone, a desolate pauper. I was appalled to learn that many great artists were treated shabbily during their lives. And so began my lifelong resolve to focus my energy in support of living artists.

I consider it my great fortune that I have been privileged to buy the artwork of superb artists early in their careers, people like Jackson Pollock, Willem de Kooning, Milton Avery, Max Weber, Hans Hofmann, and scores of other painters and sculptors. I am never happier than when I can discover a new artist whose work I admire and whose career I can help support.

Over the years, I've donated most of my paintings and sculptures to museums and other institutions all over the country. I hope the people who view them enjoy them as much as I do. A number of them are housed in the Neuberger Museum of Art in Westchester County, New York, which I created after some encouragement from my friend Nelson Rockefeller. The Neuberger Museum now has more than 6,000 works of art, 850 from my collection.

I was a young man when I developed an ardent interest in paintings. What first led me to Wall Street was a desire to make money so I could buy great art and support artists. What I didn't know when I started is that working on Wall Street can be a fascinating art in itself—and one for which I was almost immediately suited.

Now I am 94 years old. I remember how I hated my 50th birthday. Half a century old! I was much older then than I am now. I still go to work at Neuberger&Berman every day. For me, work is play. I am intrigued by trading on Wall Street, and I find it enormously exciting and exhilarating.

Although I don't have a college diploma or an MBA, I'm constantly learning. I love meeting people, and I learn something from everyone I meet.

Add to all my good fortune the blessings of a wonderful family, and you will quickly gather why these 94 years have been so fulfilling. Of course, they have not been without pain or adversity. But for me life has been, and continues to be, a great adventure.

I still enjoy making money. In this book, I tell you how I did it. My hope is that you, too, will make as much money as you need and spend it for an important purpose that pleases you and helps others. That, I discovered, is the real joy of life.

ROY R. NEUBERGER

New York, New York
August 1997

Contents

1 The Roots of Joy — 1
Beginnings — 3
We Move to New York — 6
My Family — 7
Education and My Love Affair with Tennis — 10
Business and the Arts at B. Altman — 12

2 Paris in the Twenties — 17
The Beginning of My Wanderlust — 19
Back to Paris — 21
Café des Deux-Magots — 22
In Cannes on the Tennis Circuit — 25
The Arts in Paris — 26
Berlin and Vienna — 27
Vincent van Gogh — 29

**3 From Boulevard St. Germain
to Wall Street: The Panic of 1929** — 31
Halle & Stieglitz — 33
Managing Money—My Own — 35
Hedging with Radio — 36
The Panic — 37

4 After the Panic — 41
1929 versus 1987 — 43
Lessons from the Panic — 44

Richard Whitney and the 10 Percent Rule 46
Suicide and the Panic 48

5 Making Money in Hard Times 49
Managing Other People's Money 51
Trading in the 1930s 52
My Client List Grows 55
A Decade at Halle & Stieglitz 55

6 Starting a Family 59
Courting the Elegant Marie Salant 61
The Newlyweds 63
Marie's Family 64
The Next Generation 67

7 Launching Neuberger&Berman 69
World War II 71
Opening Our Office 73
Robert Berman 74
Our Partners 76
The Arrival of the Computer 80
Economics 82
The Romance of Wall Street 83

**8 Guardian: The Mutual Fund
Comes of Age 85**
The Origin of Mutual Funds 87
The Beginning of Guardian 88
Guardian Today 90
Philosophies of Guardian 92
Quantum Gains: AT&T, Minute Maid,
    and Coca-Cola 94
Guardian's Board 97
T. Rowe Price 99
Closed-End Investment Trusts 100
Serving Smaller Investors 102

Contents

9　**A Collection Blossoms**　　**105**

Fulfilling a Dream　　107

Influence of Duncan Phillips　　107

Starting My Collection: Guy Maccoy,
　Peter Hurd, and Nelson Rockefeller　　109

Collecting Milton Avery　　111

From Collector to Donor　　114

The Whitney Museum of American Art　　117

American Federation of Art　　118

Metropolitan Museum of Art　　123

The Hoving Years　　125

Metropolitan Honorary Trustee　　128

The Art Pendulum Swings　　130

A Museum in My Future　　131

10　**Creating the Neuberger Museum of Art**　　**133**

A Mysterious Offer　　135

Meeting with Rockefeller　　136

Art Collector Joseph Hirshhorn　　137

My Reply to Rockefeller　　138

Rockefeller the Politician　　139

Building the Museum　　141

Opening the Museum　　142

The Purchase College Foundation　　145

Funding the Museum　　146

Celebrating the Rockefellers　　148

A Wise Investment　　150

11　**Ten Principles of Successful Investing**　　**151**

1.　Know Thyself　　154

2.　Study the Great Investors　　156

3.　Beware of the Sheep Market　　165

4.　Keep a Long-Term Perspective　　166

5.　Get In and Out in Time　　170

6.　Analyze the Companies Closely　　173

7.　Don't Fall in Love　　176

Contents

8. Diversify, but Don't Hedge Alone   177
9. Watch the Environment   179
10. Don't Follow the Rules   183

12   Reflections at Age 94   185
What the Future May Hold   187
The Neuberger Foundation   188
Exercise and Longevity   191
Ethical Culture   193
What Government Can Do   195
Spotting a Future President   199
The Economy Rules the Election   202
The Impact of War   203
A Little Reading Goes a Long Way   205

Epilogue   So Far, So Good   207

About the Connables   210

Index   211

Chapter 1

THE ROOTS OF JOY

From the window of my New York apartment, I spy beneath the trees of Central Park a white hansom carriage winding its way past the skating rink and out onto Fifth Avenue, carrying a young 1990s couple. The scene transports me back to another time and place, when the horses would bring my father home from work.

Here in the home I shared with Marie, my wife for 65 years, I look out on the glorious city where I have lived for 88 of my 94 years.

Through the window, I look north toward the Columbia University neighborhood where I spent most of my childhood. Twenty-five blocks in the other direction, down Fifth Avenue, is the beautiful old high-ceilinged building that once housed the B. Altman department store, where I first learned about business and trading and was introduced to the fascinating world of art.

Further downtown is Wall Street, where I found my life's work.

It seems that luck has followed me to all those places and through all the periods of my life. I am among the fortunate few who were born with a knack for happiness.

BEGINNINGS

On July 21, 1903, when I was born, Teddy Roosevelt was president, the Wright Brothers were preparing for their epic flight, and the first automobile trip across the United States (from San Francisco to New York) was underway.

My father sent a telegram to his friends and relatives:

> All is Joy.
> It is a Boy.
> His name is Roy.

Who could ask for a better introduction to the world?

In many ways, my father was prophetic. Even today, I have a great capacity for happiness, a healthy appetite for learning about every aspect of life, and no hang-ups.

My father, Louis Neuberger, was born in "Kaiser's Lantern," a section of western Germany near the French border. He came to America as a boy in the Civil War era and was already 52 years old when I was born. Though our relationship had the distance typical of fathers and sons in that era, I remember him very fondly. I recall him as an older, kindly man whose main interest was business. His early ventures were in the Midwest. I have no idea how he got there, this Jewish man from western Germany.

My mother, Bertha Rothschild Neuberger, was a nervous, troubled woman from a large, fairly well-to-do Jewish family, not related to the famous Rothschilds. Though she was born in Chicago, her family was originally from Baltimore. She had five sisters and two brothers. I have a photograph taken around 1903 with the eight Rothschild offspring and their mother dressed in all their finery, as was the custom for formal photographs.

My parents were married in 1889 at the renowned Standard Club in Chicago. My brother Leslie was born the following year in Port Huron, Michigan. A year and a half later, my sister Ruth was born in Marquette in Michigan's Upper Peninsula, on the shore of Lake Superior, where my father had established a small but exclusive clothing business, a miniature of Brooks Brothers in New York.

Copper mining was a major industry in that part of Michigan, and my father had some interest in copper. When he died in 1916, I inherited, along with $30,000 of valuable securities, thousands of shares in the Butte and London Copper Development Company.

The roots of my interest in art are probably genetic: My mother was passionate for music. She was an inveterate concert goer and loved playing the piano, which she did every day up until her death in 1912. I've been told often that she was good enough to have been a professional pianist. About the time of my birth, a German composer dedicated to her a composition entitled "Schneeflocke," later used as a teaching piece for thousands of piano students.

Hanging on my office wall is a wonderful painting of my birthplace, old Bridgeport, Connecticut, our family's home after Marquette. Among the downtown buildings in the painting is the Connecticut Web and Buckle Company factory. My father's half-ownership of this prospering manufacturing business helped establish him as one of Bridgeport's leading citizens. He also had some success as an investor in the stock market—more wins than losses—but there were some notable exceptions: I was told that in one day, he apparently lost $250,000—an unbelievable sum in those days. My guess is that this occurred during the Northern Pacific Panic of 1907.

Several years ago, my son Roy wanted to see the house where I was born, and so we returned to Bridgeport. In the early 1900s, our home at 1005 Noble Avenue was a little out of town toward Beardsley Park. Today the neighborhood is quite built up, with houses all along what I recall as a country lane. My birthplace is no longer a country house, but it is still a nice six-bedroom home on half an acre.

Gone is the trolley that ran by. My father rarely took it. Though I spent only my first six years in Bridgeport, I remember well his traveling to work in a carriage, sitting next to the driver, behind two horses.

I also remember swimming in Long Island Sound, at Fort Trumbull Beach and Greens Farm, our family dogs Goldie and Silvie tagging along behind. And I remember the farewell party for my father at the Calumet Club before we moved to New York in 1909. I was too young to be at the party, but I have the menu. My father kept it as a memento; I keep it as a clue to why few people lived beyond 60 years of age at that time. Dinner started with martinis and ended with nuts. In between came soup, fish, meat, salad, and endless other courses.

WE MOVE TO NEW YORK

I was six years old in 1909 when we moved from Bridgeport to New York City, to a spacious apartment at 25 Claremont Avenue, opposite Barnard College. The building is now owned by Columbia University and is still quite pleasant looking. Mrs. Teller of the Bonwit Teller stores was a neighbor in our Claremont Avenue building. Once when she was going out in evening attire, she needed something buttoned in the back (I believe it was her corset). My parents weren't home. I was the only one around. So I buttoned it for her. That is a childhood memory I have never forgotten.

We moved to New York because my father wanted his children, particularly my sister Ruth, to enjoy a greater social life than the one offered in Bridgeport. And he wanted my mother to have a richer cultural life. While we lived in Connecticut, she had often traveled to New York for concerts and the opera.

For my father, the move meant reducing his potential income. He knew that, but he said he would rather be a small potato in New York than a big cheese in a little community.

MY FAMILY

I never had the chance to really get to know my parents, but I am fortunate to have inherited important qualities and interests from each of them. Whereas my mother was a worrier, deeply immersed in her music, my father was an adventurer. I am committed to the arts, but I am an adventurous character as well, no question about it. Pictures of my father look very much like me. My father's particular interest in the stock market rubbed off on me. He was a speculator: He played the market and insisted that no child of his would ever play the market as he did—so I made it my career!

Even at a young age, I must have been dimly aware that my mother suffered from a psychological illness.

Today, she would probably be treated quite routinely with antidepressants or other medication. My father was kind, but much older than she was and absorbed in the adventure of business. Because of my mother's emotional problems, I was sent to the Kohut School, a very beautiful boarding school in the Riverdale section of the Bronx, right on the Hudson River. It was a rural area, with open fields and hillsides, far from midtown Manhattan. Today it is sad for me to see that neighborhood crammed with high-rise apartment houses.

In 1912, when I was a nine-year-old student in Riverdale, my mother died. I found out only recently that she took her own life. My father died four years later, in 1916. It was a sad time. We had been living at 611 West 112th Street then, near Riverside Drive, and I was attending P.S. 165 on West 109th Street between Broadway and Amsterdam. After my father's death, I lived with my sister Ruth on West 114th Street, opposite Columbia University's South Field. Ruth, who was 12 years older than I, was the person in my family to whom I was always closest.

One summer when I was at camp, Ruth visited me. The uncle of a campmate arrived in a car—an unusual occurrence in those days. My friend and his uncle, Aaron Potter, offered us a ride. I've always had an ability to recognize the good in people, a trait which has been tremendously important in my life and in my work, and I liked Aaron immediately. I said, "Ruth, this is the man for you."

Born in 1880, Aaron was 23 years my senior. He was a man of dignity, kindness, and intelligence, an exceedingly fine human being who became my closest friend. He was in the business of manufacturing lenses in a company called Potter and Schnakenberg. Earlier, he had worked for a firm that handled beautiful thermometers and cameras. Presidents Theodore Roosevelt and William Howard Taft were customers.

Ruth took my advice and married Aaron Potter in 1919. He was the head of his family, the patriarch, the person to whom everyone could turn. I respected him tremendously. I lived with Aaron and Ruth quite happily until I went to Paris at age 20.

Aaron died in 1949, at not quite 70. My sister Ruth, lived to the age of 92. We three remained very close all their lives, and I have a deep fondness for the times we spent together. I am still close to their son, my nephew William Potter, who is a member of the New York Stock Exchange and is today with Neuberger&Berman.

My relationship with my brother Leslie was never as affectionate as the one with Ruth. He was much older and a very conservative Republican. At an early age, our political differences kept us at arm's length.

Today I am a registered independent, but at the age of 13, I was proud to be called a Democrat, supporting President Woodrow Wilson in the 1916 presidential election. Two very strong candidates were opposing each other that year: President Wilson and former U.S. Supreme Court Justice Charles Evans Hughes.

The morning after the election, the *New York Times* arrived while Leslie and I were at breakfast. The lead story on the front page announced that Hughes had won. Leslie was delighted. Though I had hoped for Wilson, I admired Hughes's intellectual qualities, and so I accepted the outcome without bitterness.

The following morning, Leslie and I were again at breakfast when the *Times* arrived. Now the news was about late election returns from California—which reversed the result. Wilson was reelected. Leslie was furious. He acted as if he somehow blamed *me* for the change in the outcome. I don't think he ever forgave me for supporting Wilson's reelection.

After Leslie married, he lived in an apartment on West 110th Street, east of Broadway near Morningside Drive, and later he moved to Westchester. For quite awhile he earned a very good living running an early advertising firm our father had purchased, the Publicity Clock Company, which placed ads on the clocks in movie theaters. It was an advertising medium with a raison d'être at that time in history: All the theaters had clocks that were lit up in the darkness. Local stores near the theater would purchase ads from Leslie, and every 30 seconds, an ad for the local drug store or dry cleaner would light up on the clock.

Leslie died young at age 61. His wife was a teacher who, like my sister Ruth, lived to be 92.

EDUCATION AND MY LOVE
AFFAIR WITH TENNIS

At the time of my father's death, when Ruth and I moved to the south side of West 114th Street, we were right across the street from Columbia University's South Field, which ran from 114th Street to 116th Street. The area was later built up by the university, but in those days there was a football field, a track, and tennis courts.

I used the track for running in the warm weather; and in the winter, we had marvelous ice skating all the time on the flooded tennis courts. It seemed colder in those days than it is now, and skating was much more popular.

At the age of 10, I began to watch people playing tennis at a public court that was bordered by 119th and 120th Streets, between Claremont Avenue and Riverside Drive, near the site of the future Riverside Church. The game looked enormously appealing, and one day I decided it was the game for me. I acquired the finest tennis racket and the best shoes, and, from that day on, tennis was my life. I watched other players and taught myself. When I didn't have anyone to play with, I practiced on the handball court. In the wintertime, I played indoors in the Armory at Park Avenue and East 66th Street. I was fanatical about it for at least 20 years.

Tennis had an enormous influence on me, becoming a major part of my education and development. It helped me gain self-confidence—not so much about my playing as about my body. I was never tall (I am a little over 5 feet 6 inches), but I was strong and well coordinated and could run fast. Tennis required exactly those attributes, plus the ability to think quickly.

I attended DeWitt Clinton High School on West 59th Street and Tenth Avenue in Manhattan. Most of the many friends I made there remained my close friends throughout their lives, including Lionel Trilling, who became a great critic and Columbia University professor, and Countee Cullen, a fine African-American poet who died quite young.

But the most important fact for me about DeWitt Clinton was its tennis team's standing as the Greater New York champions. I played on the varsity team my sophomore and junior years, and in my senior year I was captain of the team that won the championship. In those three years, I won every tennis match except one—I lost against Ernie Kuhn, who later turned pro.

Like many young men, my chief high school interests were sports (tennis) and ladies. After DeWitt Clinton, I enrolled in the New York University School of Journalism, though I had little interest in the subject. I wanted to play on the NYU tennis team.

Looking back on my youthful addiction to tennis, I find it not much different from my fascination with the market. You have to make fast decisions. You can't wait to think about it overnight.

I attended NYU for the first full year but, because freshmen were not allowed to play on sports teams, I was overwhelmingly bored. NYU had recruited me to begin playing tennis my sophomore year. But, after year one, I didn't feel I was learning enough to justify staying in school. I felt that I could learn much more out in the world of business.

BUSINESS AND THE ARTS AT B. ALTMAN

It was 1922, and I was not quite 19 the spring I quit college to go to work. I went to the office of a man from Bridgeport, Milton Klein, who was a vice president at the B. Altman & Company department store. I said to Mr. Klein, "I was born in Bridgeport, and I would like to get a job." He said they would give me a job. It was as simple as that.

B. Altman would last longer for me than NYU. It was an extremely valuable three-year experience. For the first few days, I worked in the receiving department.

All arriving merchandise went downstairs to the enormous basement where large and small items were intermixed before being sent to the sales floors. I was young and strong from tennis, so they put me in receiving for the interior decorating department, which meant unloading furniture.

One day, two large cases arrived, one containing 200 antique reproduction chairs from France and one containing tapestries from Italy. Though they came from a different country, the tapestries were made to fit perfectly the seats and backs of the French chairs. The head of the interior decorating department, a tall Englishman named Callingham, came down to the receiving department to inspect the merchandise personally. I was asked to pull each chair and tapestry out from the cases for him to examine. Not only was he satisfied with the fit of the tapestries, he was apparently impressed by my energy. "I would like you to come to my department," he said. So I had the very good fortune to get out of that damn receiving department in short order.

I was moved to the eighth floor, which was occupied primarily by interior decorating—furniture, upholstery, and rugs, including a great many oriental rugs from the Middle East. At that time, Altman's and W & J Sloane controlled a huge chunk of the decorating business in New York City. Altman's rug department alone was worth $6 million, which today would be like a department worth about $50 million.

I learned almost immediately that there is some flim-flam—and a bit of fakery—in the way merchandise is priced in retail. Altman's put those Franco-

Italian chairs on the floor at a price of, say, $199 each, which would be the equivalent of more than $1,000 today. Several months later, they announced a big sale, reducing the chairs from $199 to $149. In fact, $149 was their intended retail price. Altman's cost was probably half that. They hadn't needed to charge $199 to make a decent profit. The goal was to sell out the whole shipment, and it happened—some at the higher price, some at reduced price to the few people who complained about paying too much, and some at the sale price.

This soon became common retail practice. Altman's was an innovator, the Wal-Mart of its time, though with fine quality merchandise. They never advertised that the chairs were antiques—that would have been completely unethical. But they did put coffee stains on the tapestries to give them a little history.

In 1923, the upholstery fabrics buyer left. Though still in my teens, I was offered the job. For the next two years, I bought upholstery fabrics for the interior decorating department of B. Altman's.

Mr. Klein, the man from Bridgeport, was second in command to Michael Friedsam, the president of B. Altman & Co. and Benjamin Altman's nephew. Friedsam was an extraordinarily wealthy man. At the Metropolitan Museum, there is a Friedsam wing and an Altman wing. That's how important and profitable the store was.

I learned a great deal of practical knowledge from observing the policies of Altman's management and from the people in my department. I still have tremendous respect for Altman's pioneering merchandising ideas. Most important, I learned a valuable lesson that applied particularly well to my own business: You're in business to make a profit; if you are excessively greedy you won't succeed—you will lose.

Altman's also had innovative customer relations and merchandising methods that are now regarded as classic retail principles. For instance, if merchandise wasn't sold within a reasonable time, it was marked down to cost. That may seem routine now, but at the time it was very progressive. And their merchandise *must* have been good: I had a particularly discriminating aunt who was one of Altman's most enthusiastic customers. She would never buy anywhere else.

I also learned to trade at B. Altman. There, you traded inventory for cash and cash for inventory. And I learned a good deal about the arts from my colleagues in decorating, particularly Anne Washington, an absolutely lovely woman who was reputed to be a direct descendant of George. The people in the Altman's decorating department opened new worlds for me. They told me, essentially, "You have aesthetic talent." They took me to art galleries, to the theater, and to the opera (way up in the rafters), and they encouraged me to study painting. But in no time at all, I discovered that I was a terrible painter—I quit after only six months. I had neither the talent nor the technical ability to be really good.

Though I was not an artist, I did become an art lover. My eye for painting and sculpture evolved from that period.

Life was busy while I was working at Altman's. In addition to art and music, I continued to be intensely interested in tennis—and acutely distracted by girls. Recently, a woman sent me a letter I had written to her back in those days. She had kept it over the years and had just come across it. I was amused and a little embarrassed to remember how romantic I had been in my teens.

By 1924 I was reading quite a bit, good books and bad. One of the best was John Galsworthy's *Forsyte Saga*, which among other things described the practice of well-to-do English families sending their oldest children to the continent for more education. The book had a tremendous impact on me. I decided to use the money I had inherited from my father to send myself abroad for a vacation from Altman's.

I set out for Paris in June 1924, one month before my 21st birthday.

Chapter 2

PARIS IN THE TWENTIES

THE BEGINNING OF MY WANDERLUST

My first trip abroad was an eye-opening experience. I sent myself in style, sailing first class on a French liner. I met fascinating people and ate obscene quantities of caviar.

This was the beginning of a wanderlust that lasted many years. Everything about that first trip was exciting, new, wonderful, and exhilarating. On the boat train from Cherbourg to Paris, I was served magnificent meals while I gazed out on the beautiful countryside of France.

I grew to love Paris even more than New York. I also traveled throughout Switzerland and Italy that summer, loving them both. Of course, in Italy, I went to Florence to see the great Italian Renaissance art at the Uffizi Palace. Another high point of Italy was a concert in Rome where I heard Fritz Kreisler for the first time. The enthusiastic audience demanded an hour and a half of encore before they let him put down his violin.

In late August, I returned to Paris and visited the Louvre, an experience that profoundly influenced my life. After that first visit, I would go three times a week. It was a feast for my eyes. The museum was not nearly as crowded as it is today, so it was possible to see great masterpieces without security barriers. Instead of entering by today's glass pyramid entrance, you went directly up the steps toward the glorious Winged Victory. I would then head to the Egyptian section to see the magnificent wooden sculpture of the Scribe—a small Egyptian piece that intrigued me and spurred my interest in ancient art.

It was not until much later in life that I journeyed

to Greece and Sicily to see the ancient art of Greece and Rome. I became just as interested in those disciplines as I was in contemporary art.

My traveling companion to Italy and Switzerland was Aaron's brother, Jesse Potter, who was in the couture business and traveled to Paris to see the latest collections. The opening of the Chunnel between France and England in May of 1994 reminded me of a conversation I had with Jesse 70 years earlier regarding an impulse spurred by my foolish sense of adventure.

"Jesse," I announced, "I am going to fly to London."

"Well," he said, "you're not going to fly with me!"

He thought it was a foolhardy thing to do. But I was young and eager for new experiences, so I signed on for what was then a new way to travel—the airplane. It was a terrible trip—nearly three hours in an old biplane crate. For several days afterward, I was sick in bed. When Jesse arrived in London on the conventional boat train, he was healthy, content, and perhaps a little smug.

Although my first European stay lasted only two and a half months, I fell in love with Europe. Even before my ship docked in New York, I knew I was planning another trip to Paris.

Upon my return, I gave three months' notice to Altman's. Mr. Friedsam, nephew of Mr. Altman and head of the firm, called me into his office.

"Mr. Neuberger," he said, "if you stay, we will double your salary."

I had never paid any attention to salary. Later I read Emerson's essay *On Compensation*. Now I know a bit about it. But money was not much of an interest at the time. My central interest lay elsewhere, something with a scope I could not quite define. I think it was to learn more about life, about art, and about all the elements that exist in this world and to experience all of the opportunities a person has.

This was not an abstract ambition. I am convinced that my success on Wall Street can be attributed largely to my curiosity about life. Trading securities requires a lot of intuition, something you can only develop as a student of life. I never received a college diploma or a business school degree, but in my youth, in my years in Paris, and ever since, I have been studying constantly. I study people, I study life, I look and listen and read. I have never found learning about anything a waste of time. Everything I ever learned has helped me on Wall Street. And everything I have learned on Wall Street has helped me in other areas of my life.

BACK TO PARIS

I returned to Paris in June 1925, and this time, except for one brief trip back to New York, I stayed as an American expatriate until March 1929. Living in Paris during those years was one of the most significant experiences I've had. For me it was a far better way to get an education than four years of formal college. There were some lonely days, but overall it was a happy time.

Because of my inheritance—$30,000 was a substantial sum of money in those days—I was able to live like a character from a Galsworthy novel. The interest on $30,000, at about 6 percent, afforded fairly good purchasing power. I could travel first class and didn't have to work.

In order to learn the language, I initially lived in Paris with a French school teacher, his wife, and their little boy in a large house with an attached garage. I drove a Citroën I bought secondhand for $400, and I lived the life of Riley, whoever he was.

My sexual education was soon much improved: The school teacher's 30-year-old sister, who lived in a province outside Paris, often came to the city, ostensibly to shop. She may have been a Madame Bovary type, a little bored with her husband. Her room in the house was quite near mine. At night, she left the door ajar, leading to a six-month adventure during which I learned much more about sex than I had ever known before.

The house was in the Passy section of Paris near the Bois de Boulogne. I returned to that Paris neighborhood in 1984 and took a long walk. A six-story apartment house occupied the plot, but my memories had not changed. It was hard to leave that comfortable house, with all its pleasant amenities, but I really wanted to be on the Left Bank. I found an apartment at 119 Boulevard St. Germain and stayed there for several years.

CAFÉ DES DEUX-MAGOTS

My apartment was just a four-minute walk to the Café des Deux-Magots, where I joined a group of young people who gathered nearly every day. We sat for hours and talked about ideas and art, as young people had done at that café a century earlier.

I made many friends in Paris, including a young lady

I met at the Racing Club de Paris, in the Bois de Boulogne, with whom I had a close friendship for the next four years. But though I had friends, and a romance or two, I did not have nearly the same pace of social life in Paris as I had in America. The flood of Americans in Paris included very few Jews and even fewer who were reading and studying art as I was.

Although I was living on the Left Bank and pursuing art studies, I never became a real Bohemian. Some other force was at work at the same time as my desire to be a Bohemian, though it would be years before I would recognize it.

Many talented people met at the café, but not all of them were morally upright. (It has ever been so: I learned from reading *Intellectuals* by Paul Johnson that Shelley and some other wonderful poets were scoundrels. Karl Marx, despite his utopian aspirations and concern for justice, led a terrible personal life. So did Rousseau.) One of the good people was Meyer Schapiro, a brilliant man with a remarkable mind, who would become a Columbia University professor, a MacArthur Fellow, and the preeminent 20th-century art historian. I hadn't thought much about contemporary art until I read some influential books on the subject, one of which was recommended to me by Meyer.

Meyer and I were about the same age. When I met him at the Café des Deux-Magots in July 1926, he was 21 years old and already had a Bachelor of Arts degree with honors in art history and a Master of Arts degree from Columbia. The evening we first met, he was under assault by some pseudointellectuals who were baiting him. He came out fine and, we became instant friends.

One day, Meyer said, "Roy, you *must* read *Ulysses* by James Joyce." I still have in my bookcase the 1925 edition that I bought in October 1926. It was published by Shakespeare & Company of 12 Rue de L'Odeom in Paris. I read it, without fully understanding it, yet it affected me profoundly. Joyce's manner of expressing himself gave me leeway to go back and forth in time and to be flexible about most things, which I believe I am to this day.

That same October, Meyer Schapiro came back from a long trip studying Romanesque art and stayed in my apartment for a month before he returned to America, where he was studying for his Ph.D. in art history at Columbia. He was a vigorous, extremely knowledge-able speaker; a fanatical salesman of ideas; always the teacher, educator, and scholar; and a pretty good painter as well.

I had room in my Paris apartment for Meyer because, by October, many of the Americans had left Paris for the winter, including my roommate, Herman Wechsler, who was on a two-year art history scholarship from New York University. Herman shared several apart-ments with me over the years, and we became close friends. He, too, was an avid reader. Together we took a course in book binding. I still have a number of books at home that I bound myself.

If Herman Wechsler hadn't been a bit, well, lazy, I believe he would have become a great scholar. I've al-ways thought that he should have gone into education, but he became quite successful in the arts. In the 1930s, he created the F A R Gallery on New York's Madison Avenue and wrote books on prints issued by Abrams, the highly respected art publishing house.

IN CANNES ON THE TENNIS CIRCUIT

Soon after Meyer Schapiro left Paris in November 1926, so did I. Cole Porter notwithstanding, Paris in the winter is detestable. The city doesn't get much snow, but it is miserably damp and cold. Even a young, strong body preferred to be somewhere else.

I traveled to the south of France to spend three months on the circuit as a tennis bum. I had my Citroën and found a nice little apartment in Cannes. Sometimes I lunched in a small fish restaurant with the Mayor of Cannes, which was then a town of 32,000.

I was a gregarious youth, so I met many of the wonderful people from England and from all over Europe, including a smattering of royalty, who congregated in Cannes in the winter. There were very few Americans, but there were a number of athletes including the great American tennis champion Helen Wills, whose picture was in all the French newspapers.

A tennis tournament was held every week in a different place, with Cannes as the hub of the circuit. I played in Nice for a week, in Beaulieu, in Menton, and in Monte Carlo. I joined the New Lots Tennis Courts of Cannes and played against the great Fred Perry when he was 16 years old. The record shows that I beat him in doubles and singles.

During that time, I had a delightful, mild affair with a lovely young Dutch woman who was a fine tennis player. I also learned to drink martini cocktails in a club for chauffeurs over a garage that housed only Rolls Royces. The first martini I tasted was two-thirds vermouth and one-third gin, and it wasn't very cold—quite different from the strong iced martini of today.

THE ARTS IN PARIS

After three months of playing tennis, having fun, and developing a guilty conscience for enjoying myself so fully, I returned to Paris. The 1920s, after the misery of the First World War, was a unique time for the pleasures of life. In France, as in America, one had the euphoric feeling that war was a thing of the past.

I never did talk with Hemingway or Scott Fitzgerald or Gertrude Stein, but I did know Thornton Wilder, an awfully nice man who would win the Pulitzer Prize in 1928 with his masterpiece *The Bridge of San Luis Rey*. I also met a number of young, not yet well-known painters.

Although Utrillo seemed to have a show every six months (I decided he was copying himself), Cézanne and other great Impressionists were only beginning to be recognized. A Japanese painter, Fujita, was the rage of Paris. People were talking more about Fujita than about Picasso.

My judgments on art were influenced by knowledgeable people I knew and by a lot of reading. George Moore's *Confessions of a Young Man* was a great education about the Impressionists. The book was a prelude to my later reading on Van Gogh, recounting the French failure to recognize the great artists in their midst during the 19th century.

After my return from Cannes, I went to work part-time for Alexandre Dumas, a Parisian decorating concern in the avant garde of modern wallpaper and other decor. They also had a basement full of antiques. My job paid $10 a week plus 10 percent commission on sales. I earned a modest income with little effort, which enabled me to make my thrice weekly trips to the Louvre.

In the summer of 1926, an event had occurred that cemented my budding interest in the art and financial worlds. The French franc broke momentarily from about four cents to a little above two, and then in the autumn recovered to more than four cents. With the value of the franc almost cut in half, I sold $50,000 worth of antiques and earned a commission of over $5,000. When the franc climbed back to four cents and stabilized, I had made enough money so that I didn't need to work for the rest of my stay in Paris.

Recently, I read an article in the Morgan Library bulletin called "Advice of an Art Historian." J. P. Morgan didn't write it, but apparently he followed its precepts. It included this advice: "The surest way to learn about art is to study thousands of examples and to test your knowledge with purchases." I learned a lot about the arts in Paris. I took courses in the art department of the Sorbonne with Walter Pach, an inspirational teacher who became a major figure in the art world. Under his tutelage, I began thinking about buying.

BERLIN AND VIENNA

In the fall of 1928, my roommate Herman Wechsler, who had been studying art history during our years in Paris, convinced me to join him for some courses at the University of Berlin. It took only two months for both of us to conclude that we hated Berlin. We were particularly put off by a type of prosperity that seemed vulgar to us and by an ugly attitude toward people engaged in the arts, particularly homosexuals.

There undoubtedly was anti-Semitism in Berlin already, but we didn't come in direct contact with it. In fact, I didn't run into anti-Semitism at all in Europe. For the four years I was there, I didn't know such a thing existed.

Nonetheless, I felt no fondness for Berlin. I played chess most of the time in a big cafe at the base of the Kurfürstendamm, a broad avenue analogous to Broadway. You would sit at a large table, often with strangers, and begin with a Weinbrand, a drink similar to Aquavit but not as good. This was supposed to whet your appetite for a dozen or more beers. Although the beer was delicious, I didn't really take to this.

I was put off by the excessive consumption of food and drink throughout Berlin. I have a great appetite, but I was astonished to discover that it was commonplace in Berlin at any time of the day to have three fried eggs and large quantities of bacon and ham all at once.

Herman and I left Berlin. He stopped in Dresden on his way back to Paris, while I went briefly to Prague and then to Vienna, which I loved. I loved the art, the music, and the people of Vienna. Students came from all over Europe to Vienna at that time, especially to study music and medicine.

I stayed in Vienna for three happy months, enjoying Viennese cooking immensely. There were deep snows that winter, and I loved to walk several miles in the snow before eating so that my appetite would be almost equal to the food. I recall fondly a restaurant called Schoener, quite far from my hotel, on the Sieben Sterner

Gasse in the center of Vienna. To me the quality of the cuisine there was superior to Foyer or Maxim's or other great restaurants in Paris.

VINCENT VAN GOGH

In 1928 I read a great book that changed my life: *Vincent van Gogh* by Floret Fels, edited by Henri Floury and published in Paris that year. My copy of the book still occupies a prominent place on the book shelf in my office. The printed pages are yellowed and crumbling, held together by a rubber band, but the reproductions are still as bright as the first time I saw them. I learned for the first time from this book that the contemporary world was not always interested in the contemporary artist.

Van Gogh, whose life was painful and distressing, produced his greatest works during the six years he lived in France. In 1885 he painted *The Potato Eaters*. If he had died then, at the age of 32, he never would have become famous because *The Potato Eaters*, to my eyes, is a mediocre painting. He did produce wonderful paintings after that, though, in the five years before his death. But the French did not buy his work. They paid absolutely no attention to this remarkable artist. His brother Theo labored to sell his paintings, but to no avail. Sadly, as history tells us, Van Gogh finally took his own life.

France's miserable treatment of Van Gogh, which I knew was not an uncommon experience for artists of the period, gave me the impetus for my life's work. I wanted to be able to buy the works of living artists, to support their work financially. Of course, to do so, I had to have capital of considerably more than the inheritance that gave me an annual income of about $2,000. In those days you could live very comfortably, almost luxuriously, on $2,000, but you couldn't buy art in quantity. So I decided to go back to work in earnest.

In February 1929, after returning to Paris from Berlin and Vienna, I began to make arrangements to come home to New York, determined to enter an arena about which I knew absolutely nothing—Wall Street.

Everyone knows the reply by the celebrated safecracker Willie Sutton to the question: Why do you rob banks? "Because," he said, "that's where the money is."

I chose Wall Street because in the 1920s, that's where the money was. In March 1929, at the age of 25, I returned to America a different man, ready to make my fortune.

Chapter 3

FROM BOULEVARD ST. GERMAIN TO WALL STREET: THE PANIC OF 1929

HALLE & STIEGLITZ

Crossing the Atlantic by boat in the winter of 1929 was cold and miserable. I spent most of the time on deck, gulping fresh air to keep from getting sick. I reached New York in March, just seven months before the Panic. I was determined to land a position on Wall Street, but I had no idea of how to go about it. From the dim past, I recalled names of two people my father had known on the Street. One was Joseph Ainslee Bear of Bear, Stearns, the Wall Street brokerage firm. But in 1929, when I telephoned Mr. Bear, he was too busy to talk to me, so I never met him. Today Neuberger&Berman is a major investor in Bear, Stearns.

Undaunted, I called Jerome Danzig, who remembered my father and invited me to his office at Fifth Avenue and 21st Street. He was a tall, handsome, well-mannered, kind man, the father of Jerry Danzig, who would marry the great U.S. Open champion Sarah Palfrey.

Mr. Danzig was then a private broker; he cleared his business through Halle & Stieglitz, a large, highly respected brokerage firm. He arranged for me to meet with a partner in Halle & Stieglitz at 25 Broad Street.

Large financial firms routinely clear—take care of the financing of—smaller firms' transactions. Today, Bear, Stearns, clears for about 1,600 firms. At Neuberger&Berman, though we are small compared to some of the giant players, we clear for a large number of smaller firms. Unlike Merrill Lynch, which has thousands of branch offices all over the country, we have only three branches. But we are large enough to occupy eleven floors at Third Avenue and 40th Street.

On March 9, 1929, I went for an interview at Halle & Stieglitz, and they put me to work immediately. After all of my business experience at B. Altman and my years in Paris, I once again started at the bottom. I was hired at $15 a week to be a runner, basically an errand boy for the brokerage firm. It's not the most exciting job on the Street. Fortunately, it lasted less than three days.

Apparently, Halle & Stieglitz decided that I looked like a good prospect for the longer pull. Once again I was moved up rather rapidly. I stayed at the firm for more than 10 years and became their largest producer, so it seems they made a good investment.

In those days on Wall Street, you were expected to know all aspects of the business: bookkeeping, statistics, research, margins—everything. I rotated through the company, working hard in each section, learning as I went.

In October, I was working on transactions in the Purchase and Sales department. Each transaction was recorded individually by hand, work that is now handled by computers. Today, we get a new computer run at least once a day. But in 1929, we used long sheets of paper called *blotters* to handwrite each transaction—who bought or sold what securities, how many shares, and so on. One customer for whom I recorded a great many transactions was Joseph Kennedy, father of the late President John F. Kennedy. I would write out in longhand that Mr. Kennedy sold short on 10,000 shares of American Tobacco, for instance. The whole story of each transaction was handwritten on the blotters.

MANAGING MONEY—MY OWN

The only money I managed during the Panic of 1929 was my own. Before I began working on Wall Street, all I really knew about the stock market was that my conservative brother Leslie was holding some of the blue-chip stocks that I had inherited from my father in 1916. In 1929 I was pleased to discover that my brother, in managing the estate, had also purchased a few additional odd lots of blue chips, including many of the same companies we trade today—American Telephone & Telegraph (AT&T), Lambert (now Warner Lambert), and Postum (which became General Foods and then Philip Morris). Union Pacific is still Union Pacific. Sante Fe merged with Southern Pacific, which is now part of Union Pacific.

But most of my investments, I learned, were in first-mortgage real estate bonds, which provided me with an annual income of 5 $1/2$ percent. These bonds were supposedly guaranteed. Who guaranteed them I never did find out. It wasn't Uncle Sam. It might have been God. I got rid of them in the spring of 1929 and shifted all my investments into common stock.

From March until Labor Day of 1929, the bull market continued. Except for a few breaks, stocks had been steadily escalating all throughout the 1920s. Then, just before Labor Day 1929, the peak was finally reached.

I felt very wealthy at that moment. The value of my stocks was up about 12 percent to $35,000—$5,000 ahead of where I had been in March. But after Labor Day and for the rest of September, the market slid down a little bit farther nearly every day. By the end of September, my $5,000 gain was wiped out, and my equity was back to $30,000. Something seemed rotten in the financial market.

HEDGING WITH RADIO

The most actively traded stock on Wall Street at that time was Radio Corporation of America (referred to as "Radio"), which evolved into RCA as we know it today. I studied that company more than any other. I really learned the ins and outs on a lot of different levels. In the process, I began to develop what some would later call "analysis, Roy Neuberger style."

Radio Corporation of America reached a high of 574. Then it split 5 for 1. I set out to discover why the stock was so high and so active. Nothing seemed to justify the seemingly excessive price. I asked older, more experienced investors, but I received no definitive answers. People explained that we were entering the radio age—simple as that.

But the price movement seemed to defy common logic. To me, the radio was just another new appliance that didn't work very well. You turned it on, and you were lucky to hear anything. Reception was terrible. It seemed at the time to be a far less promising product than the automobile.

Radio Corporation was run by a pool—a syndicate of speculators. It was legal at the time; but, when Joseph Kennedy was Chairman of the Securities and Exchange Commission under President Franklin Delano Roosevelt, legislation was enacted making pool operations illegal.

While my stock declined back to $30,000, Radio

Corporation came down from 574 and a fraction to 500. Because of the 5 for 1 split, it was listed as falling from just over 114 toward 100. Even this seemed ridiculously high to me.

It was time to act. When it hit 100, I sold 300 Radio shares short. This was exactly my equity on the long side (stock I was holding onto). I was now short $30,000 on Radio and long $30,000 in my portfolio of blue-chip stocks.

That was my first foray into hedging. Today, of course, hedging is a big industry with an enormous amount of hedge funds. It's possible that my account in 1929 *may* have been the first hedge fund, albeit a small one. Selling 300 shares of Radio at 100 seemed to be a reasonable way to protect oneself against the huge fluctuations.

To this day, I employ that technique when I think the market is creeping too high. I then hedge completely.

THE PANIC

In early October 1929, I was working late every night because of the ever-increasing number of transactions to record. As that fateful month unfolded—with speculation still rampant—anxiety increased, not just in my office but all over New York City. The market was the talk of the town.

By midmorning on Thursday, October 24, 1929, the market had begun a free fall that continued till afternoon, when the four largest banks in New York attempted a rescue with the infusion of millions of dollars. Watching the ticker tape, which listed all the action on the floor of the Stock Exchange, was like being at a highly suspenseful movie.

Thirteen million shares were traded that Thursday. The tape was so late that information received by the brokerage houses was hours behind the actual transactions. Many stocks had fallen much lower during the business day than brokers realized at the time.

In the Purchase and Sales department at Halle & Stieglitz, we worked feverishly into the night to record the transactions. It became apparent that millions of dollars were lost, even though the Dow Jones industrial average, measuring a relatively small number of key stocks, showed a drop of less than seven points.

Friday was equally frantic, as was Saturday morning. (In those days, the market was open for two hours on Saturday.) You could feel the pressure building every minute. Finally it was Sunday, and the Exchange was closed. I was exhausted and slept most of the day.

Monday, October 28, was nearly a repeat of Thursday. The hysteria abounded. I worked until nearly midnight, took a taxi home for a few hours of sleep, and returned to work early the next morning.

The day of the Panic, "Black Tuesday"—October 29, 1929—was worse than the previous days. Everything fell apart. I was working at a frantic pace, trying to keep up with the startling number of transactions. Everyone with whom we were in communication, in New York, around the country, and abroad, knew that the news was bad. The sense of panic was spreading fast.

When the Stock Exchange opened at 10 A.M. on Wednesday, the day after the Panic, the trading volume continued its immense climb. (Of course, even on that day, the volume did not compare to today's norms.) My own days, as a relative newcomer to Wall Street, were frantically busy, trying to keep up with the dizzying number of transactions to be recorded. Working past midnight became routine.

Part of the problem that caused the Panic stemmed from the fact that many investors at the time played the market on 10 percent margin. If you put up $100,000, you could buy $1 million worth of stock. But if your portfolio went down 10 percent, you could lose 10 percent of the $1 million—the whole $100,000. You were broke.

If the value of your stocks dropped by more than 10 percent, you were in debt. Your paper wealth was suddenly worthless. The mythical millionaire who jumped out the window in 1929 might have just discovered that the market value of his securities had plunged 50 percent. Instead of owning stock worth $1 million dollars (on paper, of course), he would have owed his broker $500,000, payable not with paper but with cash. In the early 1930s, countless people were in this unpleasant situation.

Bears made some money, but a lot of people had become unexpectedly bearish in 1928. The market by then was already too high; they had lost their shirts earlier.

I didn't have a margin account for my $30,000 portfolio. I had paid the full amount for those stocks when I purchased them in the spring of 1929. Of course, when I sold Radio Corporation short in September, I was required to put some money into a margin account. Radio Corporation had a high degree of volatility, which today is sometimes called *beta*—the amplitude of a stock, the average percentage of its movement. Radio

Corporation had a large beta, a great deal of percentage movement. Percentage-wise, it moved much faster than AT&T, which I had held onto even as it fell to half its worth before the Panic.

My portfolio consisted of conservative investment stocks. Certain stocks don't constantly move by a large percentage. In today's market, for example, a telephone company will move much less than an automotive, like Chrysler. Yet the amplitude of a great number of stocks today is much greater than it used to be.

On November 13, 1929, the first—but not the ultimate—market bottom after the Panic was realized. By then the lives of most Americans had been dramatically altered from a year before, even from six months before. We had witnessed the most powerful financial panic in American history. It affected people all over the globe.

Chapter 4

AFTER THE PANIC

In the days following October 29, the bear market continued downward, reaching bottom on November 13. It then started to climb back up, and by April 1930, the Dow Jones average had recovered by 50 percent. As they looked at those figures, many financial and political leaders proclaimed the Panic an aberration and predicted that prosperity was just around the corner. They were wrong. The market took another nose dive, hitting a new low in October 1930, a year after the Panic. It continued downward. Within another two years, the market would be worth only 11 percent of its September 1929 high. Radio Corporation of America, which I had sold short at 100, ultimately sank to 2.

1929 VERSUS 1987

Because I am the only person I know who was active on Wall Street during both the 1929 Panic and the 1987 stock market crash, I am often asked to compare the two. The most obvious difference, I think, is in longevity of effects: 1929 ushered in a long, deep Depression that did not end until the start of World War II. Great fortunes were lost. Life changed for families both rich and not so rich. The 1929 Panic was substantial in its long-term effects on individuals, on big business, and on the nation. At the end of 1929, we entered the worst bear market in history. By June 1932, the market had lost 89 percent of its value.

The aftermath of 1987, however, was quite different. In fact, stocks have advanced dramatically in the 1990s. In contrast to the cataclysmic events of 1929, the 1987 correction was superficial. It lasted for one week in October. It was caused by ridiculous advances in stock prices earlier that year, when interest rates were high. That same week in October, the bond market soared. This was characteristic. Bonds are not often my favorite investment, but it was a great idea to have long-term bonds that week. When the dust cleared, by the end of 1987, the market was slightly up, quite unlike conditions at the end of 1929.

1987 has been called a bear market; but, more accurately, it was a correction in a bull market. The value of the market went on to double by 1994, and the upward trend has continued.

LESSONS FROM THE PANIC

Even during the Panic, I never regretted my decision to go to Wall Street. Quite the opposite. I learned a lot in 1929. I studied the market and learned fast that something was wrong. Perhaps because I wasn't on Wall Street (or even in America) earlier in the 1920s, I was able to see trouble looming—while others with more hands-on experience lulled themselves into thinking the market would continue to rise indefinitely.

At the time, I was using all of the life experience I had acquired by age 26, particularly common sense, a commodity sometimes in short supply on Wall Street. I considered the Panic to be the signal of a disease in our economic environment. I also felt that we were heading for a bear market, and I acted on that judgment.

In many ways, the Panic shaped my current approach to the market: I am prematurely bearish when the market experiences a prolonged ascent, when everybody is pleased because they're growing richer. And, conversely, I'm very bullish when the market drops perceptibly because I feel it has already discounted any troubles we are going to have.

A lot of people don't like the idea of selling short. But it's legal—and often quite helpful. It provides a healthy balance for the market. Suppose only bulls were in the market. If something went wrong, there would be no one to buy the stock. When times get weaker and the market psychology is poor, the bears tend to compensate.

After being involved in the market for more than 65 years, I still feel the way I did when I entered it in 1929. Now, as then, I prefer, on average and over the long haul, a carefully selected common stock. And, over the past few years, bonds have gone down far more than stocks.

What is a carefully selected stock? Johnson & Johnson, for example, the largest company in the pharmaceutical industry. It has an enormous number of diverse products that sell in about 57 countries. That is my idea of a good company, and a conservative investment.

But times have changed. Years ago, many people considered Montgomery Ward to be a good investment. Montgomery Ward is not even tradable today. I don't know what happened to it, or even if it is still around, but it was once the second largest retail business in the country.

In order to do well, you must be able to learn from the past. And you need to look at things objectively. I learned to be absolutely pragmatic and realistic during the prolonged bear market that ensued after the Panic.

I think one of the biggest problems of the 1920s was

the systematic refusal by so many people to be realists. They wanted the boom to continue forever, so they failed to notice how much of it was fleeting. Many businesses appeared to be in better shape than they actually were. Examples of failure were everywhere: The textile industry suffered a huge crash in 1924; Florida was the site of a major real estate panic in 1925 and did not recover for many years. But people refused to see the warning signs.

RICHARD WHITNEY AND
THE 10 PERCENT RULE

You can't always win on Wall Street, so you have to learn to cut losses quickly and move on gracefully. At one point, I was bullish on International Harvester. Right after I bought it, unfortunately, it began going down, down, down—and I realized I had made a mistake. I sold it the same day, lucky to take a small, quick drop rather than a big, drawn-out loss. Like many traders, I don't win on everything. Over the years, I've lost quite often, but obviously I've won more than I lost.

Getting married to a stock can prove disastrous. The 10 percent rule is sensible: *If your stock starts falling, take a loss of 10 percent and start again.* I take this idea very seriously, and it's worked quite well for me. The flip side of that rule is not to be greedy with profits. Never try to guess the top.

In 1929, Richard Whitney was stubborn. He was the highly respected president of the New York Stock Exchange. His brother was a major partner in the Morgan Company. A month after the Panic, the Governing Committee of the New York Stock Exchange passed a resolution in appreciation of Mr. Whitney's "efficient and conscientious" labors during the crisis. "Great emergencies produce the men who are competent to deal with them," the Governing Committee concluded. In 1932, a United States Senate Committee investigating the stock market found no fault with his behavior.

But six years later, on March 10, 1938, the District Attorney of New York County, Thomas E. Dewey, arrested Richard Whitney and charged him with grand larceny. His arrest was repeated the following day by the New York State Attorney General. The case involved millions of dollars of gratuity funds owned by the New York Stock Exchange, of which Whitney was a trustee.

Whitney had made some unfortunate choices in 1929. He refused to sell, stubbornly watching his investments decline until he was wiped out. It turned out that he had used the gratuity funds to cover his debts. Whitney stole not from the public but from his fellow professionals.

I never met Whitney, though mutual friends attested to his great charm. He had every advantage in life. He was born to a wealthy family, acquired a fine education, and was considered to be an intelligent man. His brother, an extraordinarily generous man who wanted to uphold the honor of the family, put up more than $10 million of his own money in an effort to calm the situation. But Richard Whitney went to jail.

My disillusionment with the Wall Street establishment's lack of common sense began shortly after I arrived when I saw that Radio Corporation and other stocks were badly overvalued by the reigning so-called experts. That disillusionment was strongly reenforced by the Richard Whitney case. Clearly, Whitney did not abide by the 10 percent rule: Recognize a mistake early, and take immediate action.

SUICIDE AND THE PANIC

Stories about stock brokers jumping out of office windows during the Panic are myths. They just didn't happen. People lost money, and there was high unemployment and a lot of desperate poverty. But the suicide rate was not especially high. Statistics showed only a small increase in the total number of suicides in 1929. Lurid stories about supposed jumps were manifestations of widespread fear.

The most spectacular Panic-associated death actually occurred a few years later, in March 1932, when Ivar Kreuger, the Swedish match king, committed suicide in Paris, causing a panic on Wall Street in Saturday-morning trading. His firm, Kreuger and Toll, was highly esteemed on both sides of the Atlantic. His respectability was such that he was able to borrow millions of dollars from great institutions here and abroad. Then, in one day, he *lent* $10 million to the government of Italy. Of course, when one lends money, one's credit rating is improved, so Kreuger was able to continue borrowing. Finally, he was cornered. His debts far exceeded his resources. He shot himself in his Paris apartment.

When news of Kreuger's death and the ensuing panic selling reached Wall Street, it was comparable to the October 29 Panic. I'm sure I was not the only one at the time who was greatly relieved that the Kreuger panic proved to be short lived.

Chapter 5

MAKING MONEY IN
HARD TIMES

MANAGING OTHER PEOPLE'S MONEY

In March 1930, one year after I joined Halle & Stieglitz, I decided to throw my hat in the ring to become a customer's broker, also known as a money manager or investment counselor. I felt confident about my financial accomplishments to that point, having worked hard at my apprenticeship and having learned the operations of each department as I was rotated. I had also fared well with my own money during the Panic—quite a rigorous test for a rookie.

The truth is that I had done better than many more experienced investors only because I hedged. I protected my account by selling short a stock I thought was overpriced. If I had been completely wrong, Radio Corporation of America would have gone up while other stocks went down. But Radio started on a long downward path, and I made enough money to offset my losses on the long side. I was down only about 15 percent in a year when 100 percent losses were commonplace. I was worth about $25,000 instead of $30,000. Compared to most people, my losses were small.

So I was ready to manage OPM—other people's money.

Early April 1930, when the Dow Jones average had recovered by 50 percent, was a great time to sell again. I'd learned a lot fast from the previous year and could handle money reasonably well in the bear market that continued into June and July of 1932.

TRADING IN THE 1930s

On April 3, 1930, I moved into the board room, where the buying and selling took place. I was fortunate to start with a terrific account. My esteemed and much loved brother-in-law, Aaron Potter, had three brokerage accounts with the finest houses on the Street, and he transferred all three to me.

"Roy, take these accounts," he said. "You can't possibly do as badly as they did."

Aaron gave me power of attorney, which is enormously important when decisions have to be made quickly. By having the power of attorney, I was his "customer's broker": I could buy and sell on his behalf, manage his money, without having to consult him. I never liked being called a "customer's broker." I think "money manager" is a much clearer title. But a customer's broker is what I have been all these years.

As a customer's broker, I received no salary. Instead, I made a percentage of the firm's commission on each transaction. As a customer's broker, you don't charge a fee. An investment counselor charges a fee for advising people about their total portfolios. Only very wealthy families or large institutions use investment counselors. A person with $100,000 doesn't need an investment counselor. It is too small a sum. Some firms will assign you to an investment counselor only if you have an account worth more than $1 million.

When Aaron Potter gave me his power of attorney, it was a tremendous vote of confidence, one of the biggest moments of my life. From that moment on, I never solicited an account, I never asked to have an account.

Aaron had lost some money during the Panic, but his losses were not heavy because he invested conservatively. He had no debt. Like me, Aaron had paid for what he owned. He didn't believe in buying on margin, and he had kept his brokers from doing it.

Today, you can still buy stock on margin, but the margin is 2 to 1 instead of 10 to 1. With $10,000 today, you can buy no more than $20,000 worth of stock.

I did a great deal of investing for Aaron Potter and produced well over the years. Aaron was the head of the leading optical manufacturing and wholesale company in New York. In 1932, in the depths of the Depression, he sold his business to the American Optical Company for a substantial sum, which I then invested in stocks.

But it was a tough time for the markets, and for the nation as a whole. We were a chastened country. Everything was down. Many of the great companies were not even paying dividends. In the early 1930s, there was talk that the Panic of 1929 was a short-term abnormality. But as time went by, more people lost jobs, investors continued to lose money, and the nation was poorer. We were in an economic bind. Labor hadn't gotten its share in the days of prosperity. No one understood how to use monetary policy to create money artificially and generate purchasing power.

President Herbert Hoover couldn't stop the downward spiral. When Franklin Roosevelt was elected president, he lifted spirits. He was wonderful for the disposition of the nation. Yet even six years into the New Deal, we still had crippling unemployment—as high as

17.3 percent in 1939. Many people don't remember—or don't want to remember—that it took World War II to pull us out of the Depression.

Trading on Wall Street in the 1930s was very different from what it is today. The current market involves millions of people. In the 1930s, only a handful of people traded on Wall Street, and the impression was that you had to be very rich to have a brokerage account. That is all changed. Today, anyone can open an account at a neighborhood bank.

Even when the market went up in the 1930s, conditions on Wall Street never really compared favorably to the conditions of today. At the time of the Bank Holiday in 1933, the market had dropped to nearly the 1932 low. Then a gradual upward trend developed. The market rose every year until 1937 when it turned into another bear market. The Depression was still looming large.

Rallies in the 1930s were short lived, as when John D. Rockefeller Jr. put in a bid for a million shares of Standard Oil of New Jersey. As soon as it became known who the buyer was, the market staged a spectacular rally. This kind of event occurred from time to time, but brief rallies were followed by steeper declines.

It was a good time to be a bear.

I received a real education into seeing things as they are, not as one might wish they were. I learned that the market has a rhythm of its own, like the waves of the ocean. Every few months, there is a change. Sometimes a long-term investor can ride out the ups and downs. But I'm a trader. I have to be closely attuned to the changing waves. It's often a choppy voyage.

MY CLIENT LIST GROWS

My second client, recommended by Aaron, was Harry Purdy of Darien, Connecticut, who was also in the eyeglass business. Next came "Dr." Yates, who ran the eyeglass department in Macy's. He wasn't a doctor, but he looked liked one, which was probably quite useful in handling customers.

When Dr. Yates retired, he was extremely well off and moved to Florida. He always wanted to own a Cadillac. One day, he telephoned me to ask if it was all right for him to buy one. I assured him that it was.

Five years later, he called again. "Roy," he said, "there is a salesman here who wants to sell me a new car."

I asked him if the old one was still good. "Oh, yes," he said. "It's fine. It has gone about 20,000 miles."

"Don't buy," I said.

He told me later that he was very happy that I gave him that advice. Of course, I assisted him in more complicated matters, but basically, the same principles applied.

With the market shrinking so severely, many brokers were leaving Wall Street. Often someone departing would recommend me to his clients. During hard times, my business was growing.

A DECADE AT HALLE & STIEGLITZ

The Halle & Stieglitz main office where I worked for 10 years was at 25 Broad Street in downtown Manhattan, near Wall Street. It was a strong, midsized firm with clients primarily from wealthy families, such as the Joseph Kennedys. Several of the partners were wealthy, too.

Mr. Stieglitz was an extremely conservative investor. Only 10 percent of his wealth was in common stocks. He was a distant cousin of the famous photographer and brilliant art dealer Alfred Stieglitz, husband of the artist Georgia O'Keeffe and representative of the American painter John Marin and many of the best European artists. The one time I went into Alfred Stieglitz's art gallery, he threw me out. He gave me a cursory once over and apparently didn't think I had the money to buy art. I was wearing a tie, but I guess I didn't look particularly affluent.

Stanley Halle came from a wealthy Cleveland, Ohio, family. They were the owners of the Halle Brothers department store, the largest in Cleveland.

I must admit Halle & Stieglitz wasn't always the perfect working environment. In fact, during the Depression, there were about 10 partners, including one who fired people who had children because he didn't want to be responsible for the families. No, I never really fell in love with the firm. But they were honest and gave me the opportunity to get my feet wet in the business.

One of the things I found out in those days is that some money managers are just not very good at managing money. They just happened to be there when the institution assumed responsibility for a large sum. Some of these people had a conventional background and a traditional education, but little practical knowledge, it seemed. On the other hand, I know a young man who before the age of 30 was extraordinarily competent at money management for a large bank. I think it is the same in every field: There are people who are intuitively good and others who lack the basic talent.

In 1939 I notified Halle & Stieglitz that I would be leaving the following year to start my own firm. I was 37 years old, a good age to begin a new business.

On December 1, 1940, I began a new adventure: Neuberger&Berman. It has now been growing for more than half of the 20th century.

Chapter 6

STARTING A FAMILY

On my wedding day, June 29, 1932, the Dow Jones average dipped to 42, the lowest average in Wall Street history, before or since.

But in midtown, there was merriment. Marie and I were married at Sherry's, the old New York landmark on Park Avenue. It was a beautiful ceremony, performed by the charismatic leader of the Ethical Culture Society, John Lovejoy Elliott. Marie's large family and my smaller family were there, plus many friends, 150 in all.

Happily ever after? Anyone who says marriage works all the time, every day, every month, has to be pretty insipid. But I can report that by June 29, 1996, the Dow Jones Average had climbed to 5704 and Marie and I had had 64 wonderful years together.

COURTING THE ELEGANT MARIE SALANT

I first met my future wife in December 1930, a year and a half before our wedding. I unexpectedly came upon a lovely young lady named Marie Salant while investigating a stock in the Halle & Stieglitz research department. She was leaning over a file, and I must confess that her beautiful figure prompted me to make a date with her. But there was more to it than that. It was a surprise to find her there: Halle & Stieglitz rarely hired women. I can't recall another woman doing anything similar to the work Marie did.

Marie was a recent graduate of Bryn Mawr College with a degree in economics, an unusual major for a woman at that time. Her father, Aaron Salant, who became the second important Aaron in my life, believed strongly that economics was a useful background for everyday life. He encouraged Marie and her two younger brothers, Walter and Bill Salant (both honor graduates of Harvard), to major in the field.

After her graduation, Marie's father wanted her to have practical experience, and so her uncle, who was a broker in a Halle & Stieglitz branch office, arranged for her to go to work in the research department.

On our first date I picked Marie up at her parents' apartment at 1155 Park Avenue. She supplied the transportation. As a graduation present, her father had given her a Buick Roadmaster, a classy, comfortable convertible—at a time when there were very few convertibles. To put up the top in the rain, you stopped the car, unsnapped a canvas cover, raised the top and snapped it into place above the windshield. It wasn't until many years later that convertible tops were raised electrically by pressing a button.

I was delighted, though a little nervous, when Marie suggested that I drive. I tried so hard to be careful with her beautiful automobile that I received my first scolding from my future wife. She complained that I was driving too slowly.

We went to a beautiful restaurant called the Arrowhead Inn, on Riverside Drive overlooking the Hudson River. It was a wonderful evening. From then on, Marie was my major interest. I really fell in love with this miniature beauty. She wasn't a bombshell like Marlene Dietrich or Marilyn Monroe. She was more like Katherine Hepburn, who also went to Bryn Mawr and whose terrific personality is a major part of her beauty.

THE NEWLYWEDS

I liked Marie's family and friends. We socialized with many couples, none of whom exist any more as couples—not one—but a few widows here and there, and one widower.

Lloyd and Ethel Phillips, who remained our friends for life, were among the most important. Ethel, a graduate of Vassar, was six months older than Marie. Lloyd Phillips was a Harvard man. We went to Atlantic City for a holiday weekend with them in 1931 and, because we were not yet married, slept in separate rooms. Later that fall, we went to the Harvard-Yale game together. We also went to the tennis matches in Forest Hills.

These couples, Marie's close friends, made it clear that they liked me and wanted us to get married. If not for them, we might have delayed. I was in no rush to get married. But they kept inviting us to dinner—the Phillipses, the Fields, the Friedlanders, the Gilders, and others.

Marie's family vacationed at Loon Lake in the Adirondack Mountains, where her uncle and aunt had a cottage. The next summer I arranged to take my own vacation there. I drove up in my brother-in-law's car with my friend Jerry Strauss. It was at Loon Lake that Marie and I were engaged to be married.

Sherry's, where we were married, occupied an entire block on Park Avenue just across the street from the Waldorf Astoria, where I had reserved a room in the elegant Waldorf Towers. Our suitcases were already in the room when we learned that some of our prankster friends were trying to find out where we were going so they could follow us. When we left the wedding reception, we took a taxi twice around Central Park. Our friends were so confused that when we finally circled back to the Waldorf, no one found us.

The honeymoon was fabulous, driving Marie's splendid Roadmaster through northern New York into Canada, up to Murray Bay. I played tennis there and beat the pro 6–2, 6–2. We met Arthur Murray and his wife Kathryn, good tennis players but better dancers.

I took along a flask of whiskey on our honeymoon. This was considered the "smart" thing to do in those days, when whiskey was frequently prescribed as semi-medicinal. Carrying a flask was a mark of sophistication. Actually, I rarely drank whiskey, so I felt a little foolish when we passed through Customs from Canada. I had to pay a penalty for bringing whiskey into the United States, even though we never touched it.

We took up residence in our first apartment, a very nice one at 40 East 88th Street, between Park and Madison Avenues. I had preferred a location on West 12th Street near the New School in Greenwich Village, the center of the art world in New York. But Marie preferred to be closer to her parents, Aaron and Josephine Salant, who then lived at 92nd Street near Park Avenue. So 88th Street was where we started out, just four blocks from Marie's parents.

MARIE'S FAMILY

The Salants were a close-knit family. For Marie and me and later our children, family life was much more closely tied to the Salants than to the few Neubergers who were around.

My in-laws became an integral part of my life, partly because I had been an orphan since the age of 12. Marie's father was like a father to me at a later stage in life. He did a lot for me as a friend and mentor. I owe a great deal to Marie and her family.

Marie came from an intensely academic background. The Salants were strong believers in quality education, which appealed to me even though I had quit NYU after the first semester. Although I regarded myself as a graduate of my own type of university, I was impressed by Marie's Bryn Mawr education and by that of her Harvard-educated brothers.

Marie's father was an honor graduate of City College of New York. Her brothers and most of their friends went to Ivy League colleges. How did she feel about my status as a New York University dropout? I must have given myself a terrific education because I never felt unschooled around Marie and her friends. Many of the people I met through the Salant family—particularly the economists I came to know through Marie's brothers—were part of my continuing education.

Aaron Salant was a scholar and an intellectual. He was teaching when his older brother, Gabe, told him he would not be able to support a family on a teacher's salary and convinced him to join the family firm, Salant & Salant. Gabe, who had started the company with their father, was the astute businessman in the family.

To meet my father-in-law, you would have guessed that he was a teacher or writer, not a prosperous businessman. But he became president of Salant & Salant, the largest manufacturer of work shirts in the country.

It is still in existence as a men's clothing company. Aaron was a reasonably good businessman, but I think he would have been happier if he had stayed in education.

My father-in-law didn't believe in joining organizations or owning things. The Salants were not members of a club or a synagogue, though Aaron gave me a check every year for the Ethical Culture Society. They never owned a car, a house, or an apartment. They lived in one of the first buildings constructed on Park Avenue, right after World War I. They rented the apartment from plans and never moved.

My mother-in-law, Josephine, was a charming woman. In 1925 she had taken her older sister abroad, so we exchanged wonderful memories of Paris and Europe in the 1920s. Her brother, Alfred Scheider, Marie's uncle, a very fancy ice skater with no children of his own, loved Marie and me and our family. He was a partner in Max Schling florists, a thriving shop in the Savoy Plaza Hotel, and pioneered in the telegraphing of flowers. It was his idea to network city-to-city floral deliveries.

Marie's brother Walter, an outstanding economist, retired in 1995 at the age of 83. He was the oldest researcher at the Brookings Institute in Washington. Through him I met many interesting and inspiring people in the field of economics. My life was in some ways transformed because of that acquaintance.

Her younger brother Bill distinguished himself in World War II in the Office of Strategic Services (OSS). In 1966, Bill and his young wife moved to Chico, California, to get away from the Shoreham nuclear plant, then under construction on Long Island. They drove a

Citroën, which wasn't working too well. On the July 4th weekend, going from Chico to Sacramento, he was driving too fast, crashed into another car, and was killed. His widow, Dorothy Salant, still lives in California.

THE NEXT GENERATION

In 1934 my wife Marie and my sister Ruth were both pregnant. For the first time in my life, I felt helpless. Although the pregnancies appeared to progress well for the expectant mothers, I was literally worried sick about both. I was the one experiencing the problems, both psychologically and physically. I became lethargic and depressed. For me it was an arduous, stressful time, and the effects lasted some months after both births.

Our daughter, Ann, was born first, on July 25, through a complicated cesarean section delivery. Today, in the hands of a good doctor, a cesarean is a routine, comparatively safe procedure; in 1934 it was still quite risky. But Marie was a healthy 26-year-old woman, and mother and daughter did fine. I fell in love with my daughter immediately. Her only problem as an infant was lactose intolerance. She is now the healthiest 63-year-old woman alive.

Marie's difficult birth experience made me even more anxious about my sister's chances for a healthy delivery. Ruth was 43 years old at the time, 17 years older than Marie. After 15 years of marriage to Aaron, her pregnancy was unexpected. But it proved to be a cinch—she had a very easy time. On August 31, five weeks after Ann was born, Ruth had a smooth, uneventful delivery of a healthy baby boy. He was named William Potter.

I have been close to my nephew Billy all his life. He's a lot like his father Aaron, who knew him for too short a time. Aaron died when Billy was 15. Today, Billy is at Neuberger&Berman. I'm very happy to have him close by.

Like our daughter, Ann, our two sons, Roy and Jimmy, were also cesarean deliveries. Roy came along on November 11, 1942, eight years after Anne. In the interim, my wife Marie had a miscarriage.

Jimmy arrived on June 15, 1946. Immediately after he was born, we moved to our new home in Westchester, between Peekskill and Yorktown in the township of Cortland. I bought the house because of its beautiful setting and magnificent view of much of Westchester County and the Croton Reservoir. After all these years, the children still love it.

Chapter 7

LAUNCHING
NEUBERGER & BERMAN

The partners at Halle & Stieglitz were generally congenial, but I knew my future could not be at this old-line, conservative firm.

I'm glad I stayed as long as I did because I gained enormously valuable and varied experience. Spending 10 years with a large, diversified firm before starting my own firm was particularly helpful preparation for handling crises.

By the time I left Halle & Stieglitz, I was thoroughly prepared to make the move. They had known for more than a year that I would be leaving, and my departure was amicable.

On December 1, 1940, Robert Bennett Berman and I opened the doors of Neuberger&Berman.

WORLD WAR II

Neuberger&Berman began just as America was coming out of the 1930s gloom. The Depression ended not because of any successful economic policy or idea, but because of World War II. Very quickly, America employed 11 million people in the armed services and millions more in defense industries making ships and airplanes and armaments to win the war.

Initially, the country clung to the policy of neutrality enacted by Congress in the 1930s—it did not want to be drawn into another world war. But when Great Britain was in danger of falling to Germany, President Roosevelt proposed helping the English by lending them defense weapons and goods. In the spring of 1941, Congress passed the Lend-Lease Act.

Everyone knew war was coming. Neuberger& Berman was launched with full knowledge that America's entrance into the war was imminent. France had fallen, Russia had annexed the Baltic states, and the Germans were bombing Coventry. Roosevelt had traded 50 destroyers to England and signed the Selective Service Act. After the Japanese attack on Pearl Harbor, the United States entered the war. Though I was too old to fight, some of our younger partners went into the service.

In step with the rest of the economy, our business was boosted enormously by the war. We benefited not only by handling accounts for many clients in the service, but also by having entire businesses turned over to us by about a dozen Wall Street professionals, younger members of the Stock Exchange, who went to war. (We returned those accounts after the war.)

One of the brokers whose account I handled was an excellent card player. Every now and then he would add $1,000 to his portfolio. He had no way of spending his income in the service, half way around the world, so I invested his poker winnings.

Fortunately, all the people I knew came home safely.

The one casualty of World War II among my friends died years later. He was Charles Eddy, a tall, impressive man who was an important officer at Chemical Bank. Charlie contracted malaria in the Middle East. It eventually killed him during the 1950s. He was one of the finest men I have ever known, brilliant on Wall Street and fun to be with off the job. Charlie was so tall—six foot seven inches—that he could absorb almost anything, downing three martinis with little effect.

I made some attempts to join the service, but by the time America was at war, I was 38 years old, with

three children, so they didn't really want me. I joined
the City Patrol Corps, which provided routine police
service several times a week. Our group was important
because many regular policemen went into the service.
I wore a uniform and passed tests that authorized me
to use a revolver—I never did. The Corps did some good
work. I remember guarding the Brooklyn Navy Yard
during one of New York's worst snowstorms.

OPENING OUR OFFICE

Neuberger&Berman was legally founded in mid-1939.
I retained 100 percent of my accounts from Halle &
Stieglitz. My customers trusted me to give them a
square deal.

Our total start-up capital was $64,000: A Stock
Exchange seat cost $39,000 then, and you had to de-
posit $25,000 worth of government bonds with a bank
when you cleared through another firm.

For the first six years, from 1940 to 1946, we did
not do our own banking. We cleared through an excellent firm, Fahnstock & Company, which had a branch
office in the Biltmore Hotel. I operated Neuberger&
Berman from space that Fahnstock gave us at the
Biltmore. We didn't pay rent, but we paid Fahnstock &
Company a percentage of our commission in lieu of rent
and for handling our clearing. If we had commissions
of, say, $100,000, we might pay them $20,000 to
$25,000. I think they were pleased that we joined them
because within a few years we were doing a greater
volume of business than they were.

After our first month or so, Fahnstock closed its

Biltmore office and moved to more spacious quarters on the mezzanine floor at 30 Rockefeller Plaza. We moved along with them, and I loved the location. It was a glamorous place to work. We were in one of the most beautiful buildings in the city. There were many fine restaurants in the area, and it was a pleasure for me to walk from home to Rockefeller Center each morning.

I stayed with Fahnstock until February 1946. For some time before that, we had become large enough to set up our own clearing operation; but we made no effort to do so because every time we hired someone, he'd go off to war. When the war was over, we began doing our own banking and moved into our own office at 160 Broadway, in the Wall Street area. Two years later we moved to 120 Broadway, the Equitable Building, where we stayed until 1974, when we moved again. By the 1970s we could see no reason to remain downtown, so this time we moved uptown to 522 Fifth Avenue.

When we left Fahnstock, I had to get a separate letter from each account authorizing the transfer of funds from Fahnstock to Neuberger&Berman. Every one of our accounts came with us.

ROBERT BERMAN

What differentiated Neuberger&Berman from practically every other firm on Wall Street was that we were an enterprise focused on people, not an institutional, impersonal organization like so much of the Street. This was the case from the beginning; and it's still true today. Our principal function is handling money successfully. But even though we've become a large group, everybody still knows everybody, and we all work very well together. The focus here strikes me as vastly different from that of most other firms. Our congeniality is one of the many things that makes me proud to this day.

Over the years, we've been very lucky in recruiting exceptionally bright people. I have good feelings about nearly all of them. Of course, I didn't always use perfect judgment, but our people are of unusually high quality. Today, as always, they are my friends as well as my partners.

Before we opened the Neuberger&Berman office, we had bought a seat on the Stock Exchange for my new partner, Robert Bennett Berman, an extremely bright, hardworking man, seven years my junior, whom I had met at Halle & Stieglitz.

I hadn't known him well at the old firm. I was introduced to him by some of the people in the office. He was a graduate of Columbia College, where he was the coxswain of a famous winning Columbia crew. His athletic accomplishments, to me, pointed to characteristics that would serve him well on the floor of the Exchange. Berman earned a law degree at night while working as a floor clerk for a man who had a seat on the Stock Exchange. He was so ambitious that he was doing three or four jobs at one time.

In those days, being on the floor of the Exchange was more important than it is today. It never interested me, but Bob Berman felt it was important for us to have a presence. So, he became a floor broker, executing the orders.

Today, the volume of orders is so huge that most of them are handled by computer from the brokers' offices, not on the floor. With business so massive, you can't mastermind every little order to the nth degree. If you are given an order to buy 100,000 shares of something, it is because the client—whether an individual or an institution—expects you to execute the order immediately. And NASDAQ (National Association of Securities Dealers Automated Quotations system) today is almost as large as the New York Stock Exchange. It has major corporations, primarily in the technology sector, giants like Microsoft and Intel.

Berman was very successful on the floor. He was a likable man, a perfectionist in the execution of orders. He was also a good golfer—trim, athletic, exceedingly energetic. To look at him, you would have predicted a long and fruitful life.

Tragically, on June 1, 1954, Bob Berman died of leukemia. He was 44 years old. We have kept his name in the firm for more than 40 years. I am still in touch with his grandson, an outstanding research analyst at Morgan Stanley, who has developed a renowned technology index that I use to this day.

OUR PARTNERS

Bob Berman and I formed our firm with five other partners. Some were old friends. Howard Lipman, for instance, was a friend and floor trader who begged to come in with me. Howard was a bright fellow—and a pretty good sculptor. In fact, I have a nice hippopotamus sculpture of his in my apartment. Howard and I shared a passionate interest in art. I was a founding trustee of the Whitney Museum, which has always been a showcase for living American artists. In 1969 Howard took my place as trustee and subsequently served as president of the Whitney. His wife, Jean, editor of *Art in America*, was among those responsible for the marvelous Calder show at the Whitney Museum in 1976. She is an artist who, in 1994, had a show of her own paintings. They were both innovative characters.

Back in 1930, Howard and I were among the early chartists on Wall Street. We tracked our investments on hand-drawn charts. I used charts because I liked visual depictions, though mine were not as artistic as the elaborate charts Howard made.

Howard was assistant to a man named Milton Lipsher. Milton was probably five or ten years older than we were and was reputed to be the largest trader on the Exchange. But he died, another victim of leukemia, before he could live long enough to be famous.

Howard Lipman wrote a good booklet, *Listen to the Money Talk*, which Neuberger&Berman published. Howard's career at Neuberger&Berman really took off in 1948 when he brought us a client named Alfred W. Jones. Jones was Howard's neighbor in Wilton, Connecticut, where, in 1935, Howard had very shrewdly paid next to nothing for an 18th-century house on a great deal of land. (It became an extremely valuable piece of property.) Alfred Jones was a writer for *Fortune* magazine and a fine man. His wife, Mary, was a wonderful woman who was very active in the Women's City Club with my wife, Marie.

Alfred Jones was fascinated by the idea of hedging, which means having positions both long and short to protect against declines. If you make good choices on both sides, you prosper. And Alfred Jones did. He went long on stocks he thought had long-term value and sold short on stocks that seemed to be overpriced. That's the simplification of it. There are many other reasons for being long and short, some technical and some passing fads.

Alfred Jones eventually left *Fortune* to become head of a company that specialized in hedging. He had wealthy friends who invested with him, and for many years his was by far the best account in our office.

It was really poetic justice that an account based on hedging, the technique that saved my money in 1929, should come a generation later to a firm where I was the senior partner.

In addition to Howard Lipman, a few other people came over from Halle & Stieglitz. These were people whom I knew to be honest and reliable and whose skills I needed. One of the most important was Donald Hine, a "quiet blue chip," a man of great character and a certain rigidity with whom I got along very well. He was an engineer from Yale who worked at the Bank of New York for nine years early in his career. When I formed the firm, it was very important to me that he come over. He was a bit older, the only one of our original group older than I was. Marie and I were nuts about him and his wife Cordelia, known as Detsie.

Donald Hine's banking experience was particularly significant when we were creating the Guardian Mutual Fund. He helped me with investments more than any of my other original partners.

As soon as he turned 65, Donald retired and bought a house with nine acres on Shelter Island, facing Gardiners Island. He made the cabinets and furniture for that house with his own hands. Everyone remembers where they were when President Kennedy was shot—I was visiting Donald Hine on Shelter Island.

John McLaughlin also joined us at Neuberger& Berman. When Bob Berman died, John became our floor partner. We never had a very good rapport with him. He was honest, to be sure, but he never executed orders as well as we would have liked.

George Davis, another partner, was a trim, handsome, terribly nice man. He went to Yale and had a suite there because his father was a partner in Halle & Stieglitz.

Sam Wormser was one of the most delightful men I have ever met. He was in love with Dartmouth and skiing. He got married, retired early, and went to live near Dartmouth.

Charlie Simon, a friend and colleague, was one of the original partners of the Salomon firm in its former greatness, when it was run by Billy Salomon. It was an old, respected firm, and Charlie Simon was one of the wisest and brightest men I knew. In retrospect, he was not always so wise in his personal habits: He was ridiculously overweight.

All of these people came together to begin Neuberger &Berman. I was the chief business person. The others, to describe them accurately, were my helpers. My original colleagues were all talented in different ways, but they couldn't compare to my present partners, who are not only extraordinary people but also extremely successful, even in today's very competitive market. Neuberger&Berman today is superbly managed by the remarkable Larry Zicklin. Under his leadership, the firm has remained true to the high standards set at the beginning, even as it has evolved into an enterprise with 850 people handling some $50 billion and occupying 11 floors of a midtown Manhattan skyscraper. My present partners have been with me for quite a while, but none of them actually knew any of my original partners. That happens when you're still working at age 94!

We have a club for people who have been with the firm more than 25 years. Each year there's a party at which another 10 or so people join the club. We note our sorrow at the passing of any members who have died during the year. Not surprisingly, I am the only member of the club who has been here for 57 years.

THE ARRIVAL OF THE COMPUTER

When I started on Wall Street, there was no such thing as a computer. Stock transactions were recorded by hand. An employee of a brokerage firm—me, during the 1929 panic—would write out a report on every transaction. It was because of the large number of transactions in October 1929 that I worked so late every night while Wall Street was crashing.

At Neuberger&Berman, we were pioneers in the use of computers. I give credit for this to the partners I had the good judgment to choose. They were smart enough to see early in the development of the computer that it was going to be a necessity.

We purchased our first computer in 1967, a gigantic IBM machine that was a monolith of inefficiency. It cost a million and a half dollars, required a network of wires running under the floor, and needed 60 people to run it. We housed it in a separate office that was about two blocks from our main office at 120 Broadway. Despite all its drawbacks, it was more efficient than doing the work by hand. It helped us survive some panicky times on Wall Street in 1970 when five of the ten largest Wall Street brokerage firms failed, in part because they couldn't keep up with the volume of trading. They were fine firms. Many excellent small firms failed, too. But Neuberger&Berman survived and prospered.

A few years ago we spent $350,000 for a mainframe computer that runs by itself 24 hours a day in one small room. It minds its own business and does what it is told to do. Of course, now every desk in our office has a personal computer.

The first thing I do when I get to my office in the morning is turn on the computer. A good part of the day I am busy watching the market on my screen. Many of the trading decisions that I make during the course of the day are based on information I get from my PC.

In the course of writing this memoir, there have been times when I have had to turn off the computer to concentrate on the book. Sometimes it's hard to keep it turned off. Like most of America, I have become somewhat addicted to my computer.

Each day computer runs are delivered to my desk that tell me everything about my accounts. This includes my own account and the family accounts for which I trade—those of my children and the Neuberger Foundation, my principal conduit for charitable giving. Much of the time, the computer tells me more than I need to know more often than I need to know it. But it is part of modern Wall Street, where technology has revolutionized the financial business.

I think the number of workers in America displaced because of the computer now amounts to tens of millions. Statistics show that most of these people find other jobs, if you can believe statistics.

A Chinese man from Hong Kong once told me that what was inside our heads wasn't so much a brain as a type of computer, plus a warehouse. I guess today it would be called a computer with CD-ROM memory.

ECONOMICS

As Neuberger&Berman expanded, I put to good use the knowledge of economics I had gained from friendships and schoolwork. After I became active in the stock market, I went back to New York University to take courses from Marcus Nadler, who taught many young people on Wall Street in the 1930s and 1940s. I was interested in studying economics not just as an intellectual exercise but as a subject that really engrossed me. I became emotionally involved in it. I realized that my father-in-law was right—economics is one of the most important subjects to master.

Having taken a very long break from school, I finally realized the value of college courses as they related to what I was doing. Today, NYU acts as if I had received a degree there, which I don't believe I did. But they regard me as an alumnus, which is fine with me.

Marcus Nadler was a profound student of the stock market, though he himself was not a wealthy man. He taught us how to think. He was the first person to get me interested in the Federal Reserve system. He said that the most important factor motivating the market is the supply of money available for investment and speculation. Looking back at that remark from many decades in the business, I would say, clearly, that he was right on target.

I became very friendly with Marcus Nadler, and enjoyed his company a great deal. Economics may be the "dismal science" to some, but I have found its scholars and practitioners to be anything but dismal. Early in my career, in addition to friends in the art world, I began developing friendships with many notable economists. I was particularly fond of Emile Despres, a Harvard man who became one of my closest friends. I first met him through Marie's brother Bill. He was at our wedding. His standing in the field of economics was very high, comparable to Meyer Schapiro's place in the art world.

Despres had a remarkable mind. During World War II he was with the Office of Strategic Services (OSS), the forerunner of the Central Intelligence Agency (CIA). After the war, he returned to the academic world and chaired the economics department at Stanford University and also at Williams College, which later gave him an honorary degree. I liked him a great deal, and respected and admired him enormously.

THE ROMANCE OF WALL STREET

As our firm grew during and after the war, I concluded happily that I had the ideal temperament and personality for Wall Street. I operate well in the real world, but I'm something of a romantic. And, let's face it, Wall Street has more romance than the casinos in Monte Carlo.

Wall Street is more challenging and more fun than Monte Carlo. The mathematical possibilities are absolutely fantastic. Plus, I enjoy studying companies, and I love learning more about people.

I've always believed that work should not be drudgery. Quite the contrary—work should be stimulating and fun, and you should have fun every day, wherever you are. I have tried to share this idea with my partners and with all our employees. I believe our success has something to do with that. Part of the reason we have prospered while older, larger firms wither around us is that we are a largely harmonious group who enjoy our work and each other's company.

Chapter 8

GUARDIAN: THE MUTUAL FUND COMES OF AGE

THE ORIGIN OF MUTUAL FUNDS

Mutual funds evolved from the investment trusts that were popular in Scotland during the 19th century and that existed on a smaller scale in England and Holland. Although Scotland is a relatively small country with a sparse population, it was ahead of the United States in many ways in the development of finance. In early mutual funds, a group of investors combined their money to undertake ventures requiring more capital than any single investor could manage alone.

After the Civil War, European investors joined together to form funds to finance railroads and farm mortgages in the United States as the nation expanded westward. These funds had the same goal as today's mutual funds. They existed to make money for their shareholders by investing in growing, profitable businesses.

In the beginning these were mostly closed-end funds, not true mutual funds. If an investor wanted to sell his share, he couldn't sell it back to the fund. He had to find someone outside the group who was interested in buying it.

The first mutual fund that I'm aware of in the United States was the Massachusetts Investment Trust, founded in 1924. Its prospectus was based on the earlier Scottish trusts, but with some important differences. It was an open-end fund that did not have a fixed number of shares. It could issue shares to anyone who wanted to buy them, and it could redeem shares when investors wanted to sell.

One of the biggest of the premutual funds was Tri-Continental, which is now worth several billion dollars. It existed long before Neuberger&Berman's Guardian Mutual Fund. Another was Seligman. Tri-Continental and Seligman sell at a discount and are a lure for bargain hunters, but over time they don't do as well as Guardian.

Mutual funds grew very slowly at first due to the Depression. Closed-end trusts were popular in the 1920s and 1930s. But as soon as mutual funds took hold, closed-end trusts were essentially a thing of the past. They were still traded, but few new ones were formed outside of specialized fields. Open-end funds, with their greater liquidity, were regarded as a much more intelligent means of merchandising.

THE BEGINNING OF GUARDIAN

By 1950, I was convinced that mutual funds were a wonderful, smart investment. Combining the investments of many people into one fund enabled the smaller investor to hold a diversified portfolio of securities in major corporations. But there was a major drawback, too. I was troubled by the 8 $^1/_2$ percent commission charged up front by mutual funds. It meant that even before the first stock purchase, an investor's dollar was reduced to 91 cents. This seemed to me a poor way to engender trust and encourage investment.

I took a hard look at the up-front commission and concluded that it was a mistake. The only real reason I could see for charging as high as 8 $^1/_2$ percent was greed. The commission was not paid to those who ran the fund and made the investment decisions, but to the person who sold it. By this time I had enough solid market experience to trust my own judgment and to act on it.

As an idealist, I don't generally like to accept what is called conventional wisdom. I had great respect for my elders, but I learned early that everything practiced by my contemporaries was not necessarily sound. If I had followed conventional wisdom in 1929, I would have bought Radio Corporation of America instead of selling it short—and I would have been wiped out.

So, I concluded that there should be a fund that made money because it did a good job for investors, not because it charged a hefty fee at the gate. I wanted to set up a *no-load fund*, a mutual fund with no up-front commission. I was confident that it would grow because we could do well with people's money. We would be paid an investment counsel fee and the necessary commissions as time went on.

To my knowledge, this had never been done before. I looked for lawyers in New York to help set it up, but I drew a blank. Finally, someone told me that Boston lawyers were more knowledgeable about such things. In the winter of 1950, Bob Berman and I took the train up to Boston to visit a number of law firms. We found Boston lawyers who were experienced in mutual funds, and on their recommendation we worked with Milbank in New York to set up the kind of no-load fund I envisioned.

As I had suspected, Milbank had no real experience in mutual funds. For years, a young man from Milbank would arrive at my office for meetings and keep his mouth shut because he knew very little. We didn't know much either, but we knew how to manage money.

On June 1, 1950, Guardian Mutual Fund was launched. We mailed out a prospectus to clients and to everyone else we knew, emphasizing that there was no 8 ¹/₂ percent commission. We hoped that Guardian would be recommended by word of mouth. We were too naive to advertise the first issue. And there was no inducement for salespeople to push Guardian because they were not going to be paid.

Ultimately, word did get around that Guardian was a smart way to invest. But in the beginning, the Fund grew at a sluggish pace. We had a moderate number of sales, mostly from partners with large numbers of customers, particularly Philip Straus and myself. We recommended it for smaller accounts because Guardian was invested in the same securities that we used for our larger customers.

Our pioneering no-load fund was capitalized at $150,000. It took several years to grow the market value of the Fund to $1 million. By the end of 1976, when the Fund reached $74 million, we were getting orders of a quarter-million and even several over a million. We paid a dividend that year of $4.8 million, of which $3.2 million was reinvested in the Fund. By 1993 the Fund had reached $1.6 billion.

GUARDIAN TODAY

By July 1997, Neuberger&Berman's Guardian was worth about $8 billion. It is something of a miracle to me that the fund has grown so spectacularly. Although I knew it would do well, I had no idea that no-load funds would become a much larger segment of the market than the conventional mutual funds.

No-loads changed the industry. We invented a form of investment that might have looked unsophisticated in the beginning but that today is one of the biggest factors in the market. In fact, it's the motor of the current bull market because of the tremendous sum of money that fuels it.

Guardian and the other mutual funds we handle are very heavily invested. Overall in the market, mutual funds average 93 percent invested, 7 percent in cash.

Our long-term record with Guardian has been very positive. People who invested a small amount of money during the 1950s, and held on, are now really well-to-do. The caretaker at our house in Westchester, who came to work for me in 1947, made an initial investment of under $5,000. He wanted to invest more, but his wife, who was very conservative, restrained him. He bought a home to which he could retire. (He stayed with me by choice because of his love for my country house.) He and other Guardian investors have made almost 13 percent in compound interest, an excellent return on investment.

The caretaker's wife was not the only skeptic. I had a masseuse in the country, Mrs. Bennett, who bought a couple of shares of Guardian. Her husband, who worked for the New York Central Railroad, fought against her doing it. He thought the investment was ridiculous.

There were even some skeptics in my firm, but

relatively few. My partner Phil Straus was a great supporter. So was Alan Rosenthal, who had his own firm and put many of his close friends pretty heavily into Guardian over the years. He got zero from it, other than his belief that it was an appropriate investment for his friends. He had great confidence in me.

Guardian was my baby. It was pretty much a one-man operation. I was its sole manager for more than 28 years, and it was a substantial portion of our business. Looking back, being the first president of Guardian was my work of art, a contribution that I'm extremely proud to have made.

The Fund's success provided an excellent education for our future work in pension investments, including that of the Kodak company. Today, younger people have taken over Guardian. Two are running it now—and very well I might add. Guardian is recognized as a real performer.

PHILOSOPHIES OF GUARDIAN

I based my investment decisions on a number of important factors, but primarily on earnings, book value, financial position, dividends, and quality of management. As head of an income-and-growth fund, I also paid attention to government bonds.

My tendency is to be conservative after a long period of advance in the market. I follow the same hunch with mutual funds. In Guardian, I switched from more growth stocks to American Telephone & Telegraph (AT&T) back when it was not considered a growth stock. It turned out to be a great buy.

In 1950, when we started Guardian, the custom on Wall Street was to have balanced funds. Balance meant somewhere between 33 percent to 50 percent common stocks and the other 50 percent to 67 percent in triple A and government bonds. Government bonds yielded $2 \frac{5}{8}$ percent in 1950. Some really respectable people had the majority of their money in that kind of yield. That's how different the world and the market are today.

We relied heavily on common stocks from the beginning. The average stock moves with the market. Sometimes it precedes the market by a small percent, and sometimes it lags. I spent a great deal of time looking for companies that would do twice as well or even five times as well as the market. When I found a company that met that criteria, I put a larger share of the funds in those securities.

In the 1950s, the markets didn't move, and we were bullish. We tended to buy the stock of companies that had franchises and good management. We favored relatively large companies, though they were small compared to today's offerings. I attempted to do for Guardian investors what I did with individual accounts. In that, I was following the philosophy of Peter Lynch, the brilliant former manager of Magellan, which was then the largest fund by far.

Early on, Guardian developed a reputation for doing better than the market and for not taking unreasonable risks. It had a reputation for having character and was regarded as an investment vehicle rather than a gambling vehicle. Earning that reputation was a process that took years. It lived up to the name we gave it.

QUANTUM GAINS: AT&T, MINUTE MAID, AND COCA-COLA

During the summer of 1958, I made a thorough study of AT&T in conjunction with the largest bond issue in Wall Street history—a billion-dollar issue convertible into the common stock of AT&T without any premium. Usually, there is a premium for what they call a "hot issue." This was not regarded as a hot issue. It was hard to sell the billion dollars of bonds, so you could buy it at exactly the same price as the common. The bond, when issued, was selling at about $125 ⁵/₈.

I considered this the opportunity of a lifetime. It was one of the very few times that I bought on margin for my customers, and in a substantial way. The bonds were triple A, issued by a company that I respected, that provided a necessary product and that, in my opinion, was the number-one company in the country. So I leveraged. We bought up to 4 percent of the total issue, a huge amount for a small firm like Neuberger&Berman.

Guardian had a very big position in AT&T and stayed with it for months. The stock started to move in the fall. It outstripped the market by an enormous margin for the following year. The stock was split 5 for 1 after that. Some of my clients moved from being worth a few hundred thousand dollars to becoming millionaires. If I had held the stock until now, it would have outstripped the market by an even more enormous margin, because of the spin-offs. I had no idea they were going to spin off seven Baby Bells. But I was always very bullish on AT&T. Over the years we had a larger percentage in AT&T than in any other single issue.

Because I believe in the safety and profitability of diversification, after AT&T had begun its climb, I felt that we had an excessive amount. In 1959 I sold off some of our speculative position and looked for a fresh source, a new stock that would outperform the market. We came upon the Minute Maid orange juice company in the spring of 1960.

Minute Maid was then selling at $15 or $16 and earning about $3 a share. It was making a good product, we thought, a healthful product. It was a way of wholesaling orange juice. I bought Minute Maid for everybody, for individual accounts and Guardian. I didn't know of anything specific on the horizon that would raise the value of the stock, other than my belief that it was a solid company.

That summer, the head of Minute Maid Corporation and Armand Urf, the second most important person at Loeb Rhoades, came to lunch. They sought the meeting because we had an enormous position in Minute Maid. We were the largest holders, larger than the bankers. At that luncheon, not a word was said about what would happen in September: the takeover of Minute Maid by Coca-Cola.

On September 20, right after the announcement, I received a call from the Minute Maid chairman. "Mr. Neuberger," he said, "I hope you are going along with the deal, because if you don't, it will be queered." That's an indication of just how much of Minute Maid we owned.

I had to make the decision fast. Marie and I were leaving for a long trip abroad with Alan Rosenthal, who was also on the Guardian Board, and his wife Lenore. We were flying that night to join them in Madrid.

"By all means," I said, "we are going to go along with the deal." And we did.

Then came the biggest mistake I've ever made on Wall Street—a lost opportunity. I misdiagnosed the potential of a great corporation—Coca-Cola—because I knew it had stiff competition from Pepsi and other soft drinks. I simply didn't take seriously the proposition that this was a great growth company—like AT&T.

I am pointing out humbly that it is impossible to be right all the time on Wall Street. My perspectives on the potential of Coca-Cola were misguided, and I never should have sold it. I think that most veteran investors have a few regretful stories like this one.

Some investors, of course, make one decision to buy and keep it for the rest of their lives. Warren Buffett, for instance, was right-on about Coca-Cola, and it has proved an enormous success. Such successes on Wall Street, especially by one as respected as Mr. Buffett, are highly publicized, to the point where the news can actually effect further price movement. Of course, we should also be responsible enough to report on the reverses—to keep things in perspective. Frankly, I am not convinced that sticking to one decision is such a good idea in the long term. As Yogi Berra used to say, it's not over till it's over.

GUARDIAN'S BOARD

We created an enviable Board of Directors for Guardian. It was made up mostly of acquaintances and friends in the profession whom I regarded as unusually bright experts in their own areas and who could relate to this new phenomenon we were creating.

Among the brilliant economists I appointed to the board was my good friend Emile Despres. Other members of the board regarded him as highly as I did. Emile didn't write much, so he wasn't as famous as some of his colleagues. But I believe that he was more brilliant than most of today's leading economists.

At the first board meeting, Emile gave me some advice that I didn't take. He recommended that we put 100 percent of the Fund in common stocks and keep Guardian fully invested. If I had listened to him, the history of Guardian, which has always been regarded as very good, would have been even better. But in 1950 the atmosphere was very different. Morgan Guaranty, for example, was putting 66 percent of its investments into government bonds. The prevalent thinking was more conservative in regard to common stocks.

Another board member, Emmanuel Peore, was head of research for IBM in the early days. He was able to help me as a scientist, as a physicist. He would speak at the board meetings in the 1950s about the world of technology. It was an education for us all. Ultimately, IBM decided that because many funds had IBM stock, it was unfair for one fund to have the benefit of Emmanuel's counsel. Reluctantly, he left our board.

Steve Osterweis, the president of Gimbels in Pittsburgh and later one of its directors, was one of Guardian's directors until he was asked by his company to leave our board for reasons of conflict of interest. Steve was a brilliant retailer who had kept us well informed on what was going on in the enormous retail business.

My close personal friend, Seth Glickenhaus, who is 10 years my junior, was on the board for many years before changing his career. Seth was on the board in 1958 and made a fortune in AT&T. He sold it the following year and decided he would switch to medical research. After a couple of years of pre-med courses, he was accepted into medical school, but ultimately he decided to return to Wall Street. I advised him to buy a seat on the Exchange and become a full-time broker. He did, and he is exceedingly successful. We are close friends to this day.

Seth's masterful understanding of interest rates and their influence on common stocks—and bonds, of course—helped us a great deal. After he left, Alan Gruber, the astute chairman of Orion Capital, an insurance company that has had terrific growth, took over as our interest rates expert. Alan knew a great deal about a lot of things, but he was brilliant with regard to interest rates.

Herman Jervis was a director whom I knew through the Ethical Culture Society. He went to the Ethical Culture schools and was a lawyer, the son-in-law of Al Bing of Bing and Bing, who were very big real estate people. So real estate was added to our growing knowledge bank.

My partner Philip Straus, who was 11 years younger

than I, was also on the board. Phil has a great deal of ability. In the early days of Guardian, he helped me more than anybody else.

All of our board members were people of extraordinary intellect and character. Each one was an expert in a different field. We chose them very carefully.

One friend I did not ask to join the board, though he would have been an interesting member, was Meyer Schapiro, the great art historian who had stayed with me in Paris. Meyer was a wonderful man, a brilliant scholar, but he didn't know a damn thing about business. His brother Morris did. I didn't know Morris at that time, or I probably would have asked him.

Although the final operating decisions in running Guardian were made by me for 28 years, the directors provided the knowledge and practical advice I needed to keep things on track.

T. ROWE PRICE

When we started Guardian, I thought we were forming the original no-load fund. Many years later, I learned that others had similar ideas around the same time. Neuberger&Berman didn't have an exclusive. We and the others who developed no-load funds were like scientists working in separate laboratories and coming up with the very same discovery. My friend Meyer Schapiro observed that the same thing happened in art: In ancient times the same motif could appear in two cultures that were a thousand miles apart and that had no contact with each other. I remember he referred particularly to two sculpted horses whose legs were extended forward and backward in a way that is not possible in life.

There were two or three other no-load mutual funds, which are no longer in existence. And then there was the T. Rowe Price Fund, which is very much around. Not only did Price conceive the no-load idea at the same time that I did, but he concentrated even more in the field, so his ideas have probably had a greater impact on the industry.

Price's associates were not brokers. They were investment counselors with large accounts. Establishing a mutual fund was a way to take care of smaller accounts. Their concern was similar to ours: smaller accounts wanted their services but lacked the resources to benefit from the diversification necessary to be successful.

Price did well. In the late 1960s when there was a mania for growth stocks, the T. Rowe Price Growth Fund sold like hotcakes. There was even something called the "Nifty Fifty," which included companies like Avon and Polaroid. Many of these stocks were selling at 50 times earnings. Then came the bear market of 1973–1974. The stocks lost so much value that T. Rowe Price did not pay a capital-gain dividend for four years.

CLOSED-END INVESTMENT TRUSTS

Over the years, I have purchased, both for Guardian and for myself, a considerable quantity of closed-end trusts. They have very similar managements to that of mutual funds, but their shares are traded on the Stock Exchange at auction prices.

At times these funds sell at premiums over their asset value. And at other times, as for instance in the mid-1970s, they sell at huge discounts. Superficially, they look like very good values.

The biggest closed-end trust on the market is Tri-Continental, which sells at an 18 percent discount from asset value. I still wonder why they don't change to open-end funds. It would increase the value of the funds overnight.

I am an investor in one of these funds myself: Hawaiian Global Environmental Fund, selling at a discount of about 21 percent. One of my very wise partners studied the portfolio, and I bought 50,000 shares.

There are several reasons why such trusts are highly discounted. Sometimes these funds suffer from overly cautious investing. I know of one case where the manager, a highly intelligent person, one of the finest people on the Street, is so careful that his record isn't as good as it should be. I told him so and he agreed. Another reason—perhaps the real reason—is that money managers do not like to recommend the securities of their competitors.

While I am a professional able to judge individual securities, I decided, after several years of study, that there were times when some of the closed-end investment trusts were better buys than the securities they held.

One fund was discounted by about 33 percent several years ago. We bought into it heavily and went to the annual meeting. We got control of the company and had it open-ended. We kept the same managers.

I have also used certain highly specialized closed-end trusts, both for Guardian and in my own investing. For instance, the Japan Fund offers a cross section of the Japanese market at a discount. It would be very difficult for an individual professional on Wall Street to follow the affairs of so many individual Japanese firms. At times the Japan Fund has outperformed the Dow Jones index of Japan.

In 1969 the Japan Fund went way up while the American market was going down. I bought shares at 20, as many as I could get my hands on, both for Guardian and myself. They climbed to 50.

SERVING SMALLER INVESTORS

Neuberger&Berman now has a family of mutual funds in the paper every day. I served as chairman of four funds, though I personally managed only Guardian.

FOCUS, formerly the Energy Fund, is run by the Guardian managers, but it is much smaller than Guardian. One of my partners, Donald Samuel, managed the Energy Fund and did an excellent job. We acquired the fund when we took over another firm in 1970. The old rules for the Energy Fund required a large percentage in energy securities. But they suffered through a terrible 10-year bear market. We found that it was labeled as a specialty fund. We decided that FOCUS would operate so that if investors liked energy, they would buy it, but not be limited to energy.

Neuberger&Berman Partners Fund came from the government. It had been very mismanaged by another firm under the name Side Fund. The government took it over for a few years and changed the investments to largely government bonds. Then there was a contest among firms to acquire the fund. We won the contest and changed the name to the Partners Fund. It is now worth about $3 billion and is run by Michael Kassen who came to us from Fidelity, the world's largest mutual fund business.

In the early days, the mutual fund, with its discounted commissions, was not remarkably profitable business for the firm. It was advantageous for the investor who paid a lower cost for his pro rata share of the fund.

But Guardian became an immensely successful enterprise. And I believe we contributed an important and enduring social service. It has paid a capital dividend every single year of its existence. I am convinced that Guardian will be around 100 years from now.

Chapter 9

A COLLECTION
BLOSSOMS

FULFILLING A DREAM

Though I had returned from Paris in 1929 an impassioned art lover, starting a collection had to take a back seat while I attended to practical matters. First, I had to find a job. After I went to Wall Street, I met and married Marie. Then children came along, and I had a family to support.

But I worked constantly, and my income increased every year, even during the worst days of the Depression. Along the way, I made some pleasant discoveries: My foray into Wall Street turned out to be a totally fascinating journey in itself, and, to my great delight, I seemed to take to it naturally.

My interest in visual arts remained as passionate as ever, but it was seven or eight years after my return from Paris before I was able to begin buying in earnest. I started slowly, but soon I was buying great quality and quantity. Today, I have a collection that overflows from my apartment, country home, and office into 70 institutions in 24 states, including a jewel of a museum built to house the largest number of works from my collection, the Neuberger Museum of Art on the Purchase College campus of the State University of New York.

INFLUENCE OF DUNCAN PHILLIPS

From the time I first met him in 1929, I was heavily influenced as an art collector by a wonderful older man, Duncan Phillips, head of the Phillips Gallery in Washington, D.C. If anyone was my mentor in the art world, it was Duncan Phillips.

I first visited the Phillips Gallery shortly after the Wall Street Panic of October 1929 when a friend from Paris invited me to Washington for Thanksgiving. At that time, the modern art scene in New York was barren. The Museum of Modern Art had not yet opened. There was no Whitney. There was no Guggenheim. The Metropolitan Museum of Art, wonderful as it was, stood alone.

In Washington, the art situation was even worse. The Corcoran Gallery, although housed in an elegant building, was a dull museum. There was no National Gallery, no East Wing. And a boring art day in our nation's capitol could not even be relieved by a good dinner. Except for a good steak restaurant in the Willard Hotel and Herzog's, a fish place on an island in the Potomac, there was hardly a decent meal to be had in the entire city of Washington.

But Washington did have the Phillips Gallery. To come upon it was like finding an oasis in an artistic desert. At the Phillips I saw the work of many of the Impressionists who had excited me in Paris and of contemporary American artists as well. The Gallery showed a few paintings from the past, too, just enough to show that art is historically influential and to demonstrate transitions in style and taste. The Phillips collection included an important Daumier, *The Uprising* and an outstanding Renoir, *The Boating Party.*

Although Duncan Phillips was some years my senior, we remained close throughout the years. In 1955 he showed 50 paintings from my collection at the Phillips Gallery. He said that I was the only collector whose taste was similar to his. Still later, his advice helped me decide to establish the Neuberger Museum of Art.

STARTING MY COLLECTION: GUY MACCOY, PETER HURD, AND NELSON ROCKEFELLER

After about seven or eight years on Wall Street, I began to acquire art, at first very cautiously. One of my earliest purchases was a barnyard scene, *February Feeding* by Guy Maccoy, an artist born in Kansas in 1904, just a year after I was born. It is not considered a great painting, but it was a pretty good choice for a novice.

My first important painting was *Boy from the Plains* by Peter Hurd, a simple, beautiful composition. I bought it in 1939 from a gracious and lovely lady, Mrs. Cornelius Sullivan, founder of the Museum of Modern Art along with Abby Aldrich Rockefeller, the great collector Lily Bliss, and Conger Goodyear. Mrs. Sullivan's husband was a wealthy lawyer who lost his money in the crash, so she was forced to go to work and open a gallery.

I think Peter Hurd was an excellent realist, though I would not classify him as a major realist. There are some, however, who believe that Hurd was equal to his brother-in-law, Andrew Wyeth. Hurd painted in tempera and influenced Wyeth to use it. *Boy from the Plains* remained in our home for many years because my wife was very fond of it. It now hangs in our daughter's home in Santa Fe. And, to add to its significance for me, it was the painting responsible for my first meeting with Nelson Rockefeller.

Like his mother, Nelson was deeply involved

with the Museum of Modern Art (MOMA). I met him before World War II, when he was putting together a traveling art show bound for South America at the behest of Franklin Roosevelt. President Roosevelt wanted the exhibit of United States artists to be part of a program to establish closer relations with South America. Nelson Rockefeller knew the region well because of Standard Oil of New Jersey's interests in Venezuela and Colombia. I was asked to lend *Boy from the Plains* to the show. This was the first of many traveling shows that included paintings from my collection.

I frequently encountered Rockefeller at galleries on Saturday afternoons. He was often with the MOMA's brilliant director, Alfred Barr, and its curator, Dorothy Miller. Some years later, when I met Rockefeller again, he seemed to know quite a lot about me. He had learned of my collection from his friends at the MOMA. Rockefeller, who was elected to four terms as governor of New York before he became vice president of the United States, had a great interest in modern art, and a large collection, most of it now in Albany, New York's capital. Paintings from his collection were shown at the Neuberger Museum in September 1996.

I was a slow, careful collector in the late 1930s, but each year I bought more than I had the previous year. By 1941 I had become an accomplished collector, and I was buying at an ever-accelerating pace. Much of what I bought was considered avant garde in those days, although today they are highly admired contemporary pieces.

Roy R. Neuberger, a formal portrait shot in the early 1950s. (Photo by Berenice Abbott.)

Born in Bridgeport, Connecticut, Roy as a three-month-old infant. (Photo by Haley, Bridgeport, Connecticut.)

Roy's mother's family, the Rothschilds, in 1903. Bertha Rothschild Neuberger, then pregnant with Roy, is at the far right.

Roy at age 10, June 1914.

Roy's beloved older sister Ruth
and brother-in-law Aaron
Potter in Atlantic City, 1920s.

Roy's apartment building in Paris at 119 Boulevard St. Germain, where he lived from 1926 to 1928. (Photo by Alison Harris, Paris, France, 1993.)

Inside the same left bank Paris apartment, 1928.

Traveling through Switzerland in
the mid-1920s.

In his Citroën; Paris, 1925.

Roy Neuberger's two great passions — art and finance. Here, looking through paintings, 1950s.

And, in the boardroom of Neuberger&Berman's former office at 522 Fifth Avenue. (Photo by Geoffrey Clements Photography.)

A first-class tennis player, Roy in the early 1950s, three decades after he defeated young Fred Perry.

Son Roy S. as a young boy.

The Neuberger family (minus Jimmy). Clockwise (from center): Roy R., Ann, Roy S., and Marie.

Roy and Marie, 1951.

The Neuberger children: Jimmy, Roy S., and Ann early 1950s.

Roy with Mark Rockefeller, Nelson's son, at a 1996 reception at the Neuberger Museum. (Photo courtesy of Neuberger Museum of Art.)

Roy receives the Distinguished Service Medal in April 1993 from Westchester County Executive Andrew P. O'Rourke. (Photo by Jim Frank, Neuberger Museum of Art.)

With Happy Rockefeller, 1996. (Photo courtesy of Neuberger Museum of Art.)

Roy pictured with the Willem de Kooning *Marilyn Monroe*.

Neuberger family snapshot. Clockwise (from center): Roy S., Roy R., Marie, Jimmy, and Ann.

Roy and Marie at a Metropolitan Museum of Art reception.

Roy accepting an award for Marie and himself from the League of Women Voters. (Photo copyright © 1996 by Peter Wing; all rights reserved.)

Standing near Henry Moore's *Large Two Forms*, outside the Neuberger Museum of Art on the Purchase College campus of the State University of New York, 1987. (Photo courtesy of Neuberger Museum of Art.)

At Purchase College, with Chancellor Wharton (left), and President Grebstein (right). (Photo by Salderelli-Weiner.)

Roy standing in front of
Will Barnet's painting *Portrait
of Roy R. Neuberger, 1978.*
(Photo by Myles Aronowitz.)

Roy and Marie vacationing. (Photo by Alvin Coleman.)

Roy blowing out the candles at his ninetieth birthday party with Roy S., 1993.

The Neuberger family: children and grandchildren at Roy and Marie's fiftieth wedding anniversary, 1982.

(Photo by Peter Fink.)

COLLECTING MILTON AVERY

My affection for Milton Avery dates back to 1940, when I purchased his painting *Checkerboard*. Three years later, while visiting Milton and his wife, Sally, at their home, I bought one of his most important works, *Gaspe Landscape*, a painting I have always loved. It hangs in my apartment to this day.

I became very close to the Averys. Sally was a remarkable, extremely bright person. In addition to being Milton's wife, she was truly his best friend. She believed so strongly in his gift that she worked tirelessly to help him attain his current position of significance among 20th-century artists.

Avery was an American artist who first visited France in 1952, when he was 67. I believe that was his only trip to France, but he had the 20th-century French touch nonetheless—the refined taste of French artists, which I admire. American art is quite often more rugged. Milton was not rugged except in one painting: a portrait of himself. Notwithstanding my preference for the French touch, I am crazy about that self-portrait, which also hangs in my apartment. I enjoy looking at it every morning as I leave for work.

Milton Avery's lasting contribution to art was his penchant for simplicity. That's what abstraction is all about. Of course, Milton's composition and sense of color were absolutely terrific as well.

More than 95 percent of my collection has been purchased from dealers, *Gaspe Landscape* being a notable exception. I bought Jackson Pollock's *Number 8*,

1949 from the prominent dealer Betty Parsons at a time when Pollock was so short of cash that she waived her commission.

One of the best and most distinguished dealers I met was Paul Rosenberg, whose family was very important in French art. He began representing Milton Avery shortly after I purchased *Gaspe Landscape*. Rosenberg had great understanding of Avery's work and made it possible for me to really appreciate every painting I bought. In 1943 I purchased only one Avery painting, *Young Artist*, from Paul Rosenberg. Eight years later, I bought 52 Averys from him in one day.

In 1948 I bought 46 Averys at one time from Valentine Dudensing. Again, I knew every single painting extremely well. Dudensing was a wise dealer with a great eye for art. He taught me a lot. Often he would turn paintings upside down for my viewing. His theory was that if they were still good, their artistry was verified. Strangely, it worked. I did it often for many years.

When I bought the Averys from Dudensing, he had already retired as a dealer to live abroad, but he came back to clean out his warehouse. I also bought a few other pieces from him, but, foolishly, I passed up a Picasso—a Harlequin sculpture I fell in love with and could have acquired for $1,500. I didn't buy it because I had positioned myself, in my mind and publicly, as a collector of contemporary American artists.

In truth, I had been buying the works of artists who were living in America, including a lot of Europeans who were residing here. And, occasionally, I bought pieces by non-Americans who never lived here.

Dudensing offered me the 46 Averys at what seemed to be a reasonable price. He preferred selling the entire collection to me at a discount, rather than breaking it up and making a bigger profit with several dealers. Selling the paintings one by one would have made him a dealer again; and he was retired, finished being a dealer.

I immediately phoned Sally Avery. When a collector owns a great many paintings by one artist, he is bound to have an important impact on the artist's life. Sam Kootz, another influential dealer, owned a great many Carl Holtys and Byron Brownes, which was bad for both artists. Kootz could compete with them when they sold later works. I could have interfered with Avery's future attempts to sell his art if I had wanted to. But if I undersold him, I would undermine his career. The Averys trusted me because they knew I would not sell his paintings. In fact, I would later assist his career by donating many of his paintings to major museums.

So I asked Sally Avery if she would mind if I bought the body of work. She said she would like me to buy it, and so I happily did.

I have no idea how much Dudensing and Rosenberg had paid the Averys for the paintings. I do know that there was an arrangement whereby, when a painting was sold, the dealer would give Avery an additional payment. I am guessing that it was about 10 percent. The Averys got a little bit of the check I gave to Dudensing and a little bit of the check I gave to Rosenberg.

My experience on Wall Street made it possible for me to be comfortable buying a lot of art at once. In my investment firm, when we like a security after careful analysis, we buy a modest quantity. Sometimes after the purchase, we will find that we like it *very* much. If a large quantity of the stock then becomes available, and we are still enthusiastic about its value and its future, we will buy in quantity quickly, even though the day before we had no such plan and no knowledge that the stock would be available.

I did this once with a company that I had studied carefully and ultimately loved for its value. A large investment firm decided to get rid of its stock when it was selling at 13 ³/₄. I won't name the institution because I wouldn't want to advertise their rather large mistake. Within a few years, I sold the stock for cash at $35 a share.

The same principle applied to my purchase of the Avery paintings. I was already crazy about Avery's work, I trusted the dealer, and the timing was right. All told, I bought more than 100 Milton Avery oils, water colors, and drawings. Thirty-three are in the Neuberger Museum. I have given more than 50 to other museums.

FROM COLLECTOR TO DONOR

In the spring of 1944, I was astonished to receive a letter from the Museum of Modern Art asking if I would open my home to their contributing members. I was pleased that my collection was the only one chosen by the MOMA for its benefactors to visit, and, of course, I was happy to receive them.

When the day for the viewing arrived, I raced home from the office to welcome the guests. In those days the market closed at 3 P.M., an hour earlier than today. Rather breathlessly, I made it home by 3:30.

Many of my guests had arrived. One or two had

looked at my paintings and already gone, including a young man, then 34 years old, who, like me, was an enthusiastic collector of modern abstract art—Nelson Rockefeller. He knew a little about me from the art show that had traveled to South America—it had included my Peter Hurd painting. This was Rockefeller's first look at a larger part of my collection.

It was an exciting event for me; but, while the guests were viewing the paintings, I overheard one lady say, "I don't know why they wanted to see the Neuberger collection. I have a much better collection." She was right; she did. The speaker was Adelaide Milton de Groot, who was past 90 at the time. She gave her collection to the Metropolitan, where it became embroiled in one of the great art controversies of the century.

At the time of the visit to my apartment by Mrs. de Groot and the other MOMA benefactors, I had developed a large collection of works in a relatively short time, mostly by young, new, American artists. I owned paintings by Peter Hurd, Ben Shahn, Max Weber, George L. K. Morris, John Marin, Jacob Lawrence, Darrel Austin, Stuart Davis, Jack Levine, Rufino Tamayo, William Gropper, Abraham Rattner, Marsden Hartley, Ralston Crawford, and, of course, my favorite contemporary artist, Milton Avery.

It is risky and very speculative to make judgments about newfound artists. This has been so throughout history, with some possible exceptions, such as in Italy during the Renaissance. I think the Medici knew they had a sure thing when they bought Michelangelo.

Sometime in the 1940s, I was told that the Brooklyn Museum was being neglected by the public. Although the Museum was world-famous for its collection of Egyptian art and great Winslow Homer watercolors, it had very few contemporary paintings. They needed to expand their 20th-century collection. This seemed like a good place to start donating art. In 1946 I gave four paintings to the Brooklyn Museum. A few years later I sent a check to buy a wonderful Milton Avery, *Sunset*, from a gallery. The painting still hangs in the Museum. Over the years, I was pleased to give to the museum many other works of art. The Brooklyn Museum is an important part of New York City's cultural life that's often overlooked because Manhattan museums steal the show.

The year after my first gift to the Brooklyn Museum, I gave four paintings to Williams College in Williamstown, Massachusetts, for the first of many exhibitions of my collection at educational institutions. Long before the Neuberger Museum of Art was created, I donated 60 Averys to colleges and museums around the country. I am never happy about parting with an Avery, but I had more than 100 of them.

I continued buying until 1993, when I reached my 90th birthday.

Although I have been solicited many times, I have never sold a painting by a living artist. I have not collected art as an investor would. I collect art because I love it. I like to share my passionate interest in art by donating paintings, helping museums and colleges exhibit art, and lending art from my collection for traveling shows. I collect art, I exhibit it, I donate it, but I don't sell it.

As it happened, I collected works of American artists during a time when those works appreciated in value enormously, more so than ever before in our history. There were some first-class, 19th-century, American artists, but their work didn't appreciate in price the way 20th-century art has.

THE WHITNEY MUSEUM OF AMERICAN ART

Mrs. Gertrude Vanderbilt Whitney, a sculptor and prominent collector of 19th-century, American art, loved artists and was an early inspiration for what would become modern American art. In 1931 she founded the Whitney Museum as a home for her collection and as a haven for young, experimental artists, many of whom were a step ahead of their time. The Whitney began as a small museum at 8 West 8th Street in New York City's Greenwich Village. It grew very quickly and, in 1954, moved uptown to more spacious quarters made available by the MOMA on West 54th Street. The inaugural show for this new building consisted of 100 paintings from my collection. Milton Avery designed the catalog cover.

Ultimately, the trustees of the Whitney decided they wanted to get out of the shadow of the great MOMA. They bought a corner property (half a block on Madison Avenue but only 100 feet on East 75th Street) where, in 1966, the current Whitney Museum was built. The space was not large enough then, and it is certainly not large enough now.

After Mrs. Whitney's death, some friends and I concluded that the Whitney needed long-term financial help to keep it going. We founded Friends of the Whitney Museum for that purpose, and I became one of the first outside trustees on an enlarged governing board of trustees.

My friend and business partner, Howard Lipman, who was more deeply involved in the Whitney than I was, served a long and distinguished term as its president. As for me, I realize now that I may have remained active with the Whitney for a bit too long. I became identified solely as a collector of American art. Although I am an ardent fan of many American artists, my interest in the art world is in fact broader.

AMERICAN FEDERATION OF ART

Created in 1909 by New York's newly elected Senator Elihu Root, the American Federation of Art (AFA) quickly became the most important national art association. Although it included some individual members, the principal members were museums and other institutions. Through the AFA, stronger museums could help weaker ones. Large museums, the Metropolitan, for example, have much more art than they can display at any one time. Their basements are full of art they would like the public to see. It benefits everyone when the larger museums can mount traveling exhibitions.

Elihu Root, an important character in law, finance, and government who would later win the Nobel Peace Prize, wanted America to have the great London art collection of J. P. Morgan's father, who had died in Great Britain in 1893. Working through the AFA, Root succeeded in having American tariff laws changed to exempt importing works of art.

Removal of the tariff opened the door for a great movement of art from Europe to the United States—especially from France, Italy, and England—including the Morgan collection. That is why New York City has four Vermeers in the Metropolitan and three in the Frick Museum and why so much French Impressionist art is in private American collections and American museums.

The AFA also helped introduce American art to Europe at a time when American artists were virtually unknown outside the United States. It was possible to give a tax-deductible gift to the AFA of a work of American art that would then go abroad. This was the beginning of American art being shown in Europe.

I became active in the AFA half a century ago, and I was probably the most energetic layman in the country in regard to living artists and American art institutions. I was deeply immersed in buying art and in the activities of several museums.

At the AFA 1946 spring meeting in Baltimore, I was invited to become treasurer of the organization. That post, I quickly discovered, was more like acting president. The president lived in Minnesota and only got involved when he traveled east. It was only a short time before I became the president.

Although the AFA was originally headquartered in Washington, D.C., most of its work was done in New York, particularly after I became president. We closed the Washington office and moved into temporary quarters in a Manhattan building owned by the National Academy of Design. Soon I was able to make a terrific buy on 41 East 65th Street, a building in a beautiful neighborhood, which still serves as the AFA's national headquarters.

I had to raise $450,000 for the purchase and renovation of the building—$225,000 to buy it and an equal amount to fix it up for our purposes. Jack Kaplan, one of the AFA's most consistent and generous donors through his New York Foundation, gave us $100,000. The Rockefeller Foundation contributed $25,000; and a good friend, Charlie Cunningham, director of the Wadsworth Atheneum Museum in Hartford, one of the earliest museums of modern American art, matched my own $25,000. Building on these gifts, we managed to raise the rest of the money for the new headquarters.

The building also became a home for several other nonprofit art institutions, including the Archives of American Art and an architects' organization. They stayed in our building for much less than it would have cost them elsewhere.

Part of my job as president of the AFA was meeting with museum directors and curators. It took me a while to recognize what tremendous personal dividends accrued from the hard work I put into the organization. By far the most exciting aspect of those dividends was the opportunity to know the wonderful people who ran the museums: at the MOMA, Alfred Barr, Rene D'Harnoncourt, and James Soby; at the Whitney, Lloyd Goodrich and Jack Baur; at the Brooklyn, Ed Schenck; at the Metropolitan, all the distinguished directors over the years—Francis Henry Taylor, James Rorimer, Thomas Hoving, and, especially, in recent years, Philippe de Montebello. And that is just in New York alone. There was Grace McCann Morley in San Francisco,

Adelyn Breeskin in Baltimore, John Walker and J. Carter Brown at the National Gallery, and many others.

I also enjoyed the opportunity to travel around the country, helping bring about a cultural renaissance where it was most needed. In 1949 Sam Kootz put together an exhibition of Picasso at the Neiman-Marcus department store in Dallas. Not a single Picasso was bought.

We mobilized to raise art awareness in Texas, recognizing that Texas was on the make financially, though backward culturally. The AFA held a major convention in Houston, bringing in distinguished art scholars. We made quite a splash. In the course of the next two decades, there were not enough Picassos to satisfy the enthusiastic Texas collectors who gobbled them up.

AFA's traveling art exhibitions, which began immediately after the group's formation in 1909, were created specifically to bring great art to smaller museums that lacked the resources to mount similar shows on their own. Carter Brown, who until 1995 was director of the National Gallery of Art in Washington, previously headed the highly successful AFA exhibition committee.

In 1952, when my predecessor Hudson Walker was president of the AFA, he arranged for a three-month show of works from my collection to take place at the Walker Art Institute, a major art museum in Minneapolis. The AFA also sent some of my Louis Michel Eilshemius paintings all over the country. Eilshemius was an extremely prolific artist whose works I own in abundance.

The most important loan I made to the AFA was two paintings for a 1952 show in New Delhi, India: a marvelous 1949 Jackson Pollock and a 1913 Lyonel Feininger, which in my opinion is a masterpiece. Both paintings now belong to the Neuberger Museum of Art.

The AFA published what I strongly believe was one of the world's great art magazines, *The Magazine of Art*, which featured historically important articles by out-standing scholars. Financial problems forced the closing of the magazine in May 1953. It cost $15,000 a year, which was a lot then. I had put up $7,500 to keep it going but was unable to do more at that moment. It went under, much to my deep regret. I attribute the bout of depression I suffered around that time primarily to my despair about the folding of that magnificent magazine.

As I was prepared to leave the presidency of the American Federation of Art, I wanted to create an endowment. Once again, Jack Kaplan came through for the organization with a very helpful gift of $100,000.

Subsequently I recommended that Jack Kaplan's wife be the new president of the American Federation of Arts. She was a charming and elegant woman who was liked by everybody. She had great aesthetic taste but, it later seemed, very little business sense. Heading an organization like the AFA is like running a business—a non-profit business, but still a business.

Nonetheless, the major achievements of the AFA remain of profound significance to our culture. When I began collecting, there was very little 20th-century American art and only a handful of individual collectors. One could view a little modern American art only in the large cities, at the Metropolitan Museum in New York, the Phillips Gallery in Washington, and museums in Cleveland, Boston, and Philadelphia. Many of today's important museums were created just in the past 50 years. The AFA has played a leading role in building bridges from one museum to another, large and small, and in bringing art to the people. That is an accomplishment in which everyone involved with the AFA can take great pride.

METROPOLITAN MUSEUM OF ART

For 33 years my family and I lived in a 14-room apartment on the eighth floor of 993 Fifth Avenue, between 80th and 81st Streets in New York City, right across the street from the Metropolitan Museum of Art (the Met). We frequently entertained visiting artists and curators. In the early 1960s, when James Rorimer was director of the Metropolitan, he often came across the street for a chat about Met affairs.

I have always felt a special love for the Metropolitan Museum. It is a treat to go there because, even though it is such a huge place, it still pays attention to the individual. The Met holds 5,000 years of art, a vast encyclopedia of civilization and culture, tended by a series of remarkable curators and directors.

I look back with some reverence at Robert Beverly Hale, the extraordinary curator of American art at the Metropolitan from 1957 to 1966 (he had been assistant curator from 1949 to 1957). He had a great deal of trouble acquiring contemporary works because of a reactionary acquisitions committee that had little tolerance for abstract art. I was quite interested in abstract art, and I discovered that a donation of cash to buy a particular work was more likely to be accepted than the actual work itself. Around 1950, I wrote checks so the Met could buy paintings by George L. K. Morris, Hans Hofmann, and other abstract artists.

In 1968, the Met asked me to study their finances, giving me all the particulars from the previous 18 years. I concluded at that time that their finances were inadequate for a great institution. Today, they are in remarkably good shape, thanks to the superb leadership of Philippe de Montebello, the director, and Bill Luers, the president.

James Rorimer offered to name the American Wing after me if I would give them the bulk of my collection. The Wing would showcase 19th- and 20th-century American art. I didn't accept the offer because, apart from a couple of James Quidors and some works by Thomas Cole, I had very few pieces from the 19th century. Rorimer's offer, made in the last year of his life, flattered me but was highly impractical. I was delighted that he wanted my collection, but it's not really contextually compatible with the American Wing, which is largely historical.

America in the 19th century was noted more for building railroads and other business exploits than for art. Because we are a young nation, the United States has always had to play cultural catch-up with Europe. We did have some excellent 19th-century artists whose work can now be seen in the Met's American Wing. Church was a great landscape painter, as was Albert Bierstadt. Thomas Moran did wonderful paintings of the West. Some of the primitive artists whose works appeared to be awkward, and were available for as little as $1, are now highly esteemed.

Rorimer died in 1962, just six months after his offer. I knew he wasn't well when we were lunching at the Met one day and he was having trouble coordinating his movements, a sad symptom of his physical decline. His sudden death was painful to those of us who knew and admired him, but it did not come as a surprise.

THE HOVING YEARS

Thomas Hoving served 10 exciting, turbulent years as director of the Metropolitan, from 1967 to 1977. He was exceedingly young when he took the job. Often, early in his reign, he would come across the street from the Met to my apartment to talk things over, as Rorimer had done.

Hoving was probably the director best known to the public because he had a spectacular career. A curator of medieval art with the Met, he became Commissioner of Parks for New York City in 1966 in the administration of Mayor John Lindsay. He revolutionized Central Park by closing it to automobiles for part of the day, making the park's roads accessible to the public for cycling, roller skating, and such, and demonstrating that automobiles were not the kingpin in Manhattan. A lot of people were angered because the closing would cause traffic conditions to temporarily worsen in some parts of the city. But most of what Hoving did for Central Park still prevails, indicating his good judgment.

When he returned to the Met as director, Hoving ushered in an era of physical change that made the Museum a much larger institution. He helped select the expansion architects and worked closely with them. The plans that he laid are still being put into effect.

One of the changes Hoving wanted was a new wing on the western side of the building to house the collection of Bobby Lehman, which had just been acquired by the Met. He asked me to go down to City Hall with him to get the approval to build. It was a controversial plan for two reasons: First, it involved annexing park land. Second, there was a strong feeling that the Lehman collection should be left in the 54th Street building where it was originally placed. There are other museums that have off-site buildings: Several buildings of the Louvre are located in other areas of Paris. The Met also has its own precedent—its great medieval collection located in the Cloisters at the northern tip of Manhattan.

But ultimately, the new wing did get City approval. The wing has been significant because it shows exhibitions that are appropriate to its architecture, including the wonderful Lehman collection. And the separate building on 54th Street is now partly replicated in the main Museum.

To his great credit, Hoving imagined the museum to be what it is today: an encyclopedia of art. At the Met, you can see the history of civilization.

But Hoving also made some arrogant, questionable decisions. Debates still rage about the vase he bought for the Greek and Roman department for $1 million— more than anyone had ever paid for a piece of ancient art. Previously, $250,000 was the absolute top price for that kind of art. And the vase was bought under peculiar circumstances, without a clear title.

Tom Hoving was also determined to buy a very expensive Velazquez painting. The enormous sum asked for the painting was $5.7 million. The Met did not have anywhere near $5.7 million available for new acquisitions. But Hoving didn't ask the trustees to raise the money for the Velazquez, nor did he discuss with them his plans to acquire it. Instead, he raised the cash by selling to the Marlborough Gallery a Van Gogh and a Rousseau from the collection of Adelaide Milton de Groot (the woman who, in 1944, said her collection was better than mine).

The Met had many Van Goghs, including one given to them by Ambassador Walter Annenberg that was quite similar to the de Groot that Hoving sold. But the Rousseau was a different matter. Henri Rousseau, one of the great primitives of modern times, was a much less prolific artist, and the Met had only one Rousseau besides the very fine painting donated by Adelaide de Groot. Rousseaus are so rare in the world that you don't give them away without serious consultation. The MOMA has two, and the Met should have two.

Of course, Velazquez is also very rare. But the Frick Museum is rich in works by Velazquez. One has only to walk down Fifth Avenue, a few blocks from the Met, to see them. Furthermore, selling paintings from the De Groot collection, I believe, was a breach of faith. Every museum wanted the De Groot collection, but she gave it to the Met.

I myself would have taken a different route, a tactic often used by the National Gallery in London. When they want a highly coveted work of art, like the fragment of a DaVinci they bought recently, they sponsor a public subscription. If the Met had advertised as such, they could have raised a lot of money.

Hoving's sale of the Van Gogh and the Rousseau became a cause célèbre. I felt so strongly about it that I went to the Marlborough Gallery, without anyone knowing about it, and asked, "If the Metropolitan wanted to get those pictures back, would you accommodate them?" They said they would. I immediately called Douglas Dillon, who was then president of the Metropolitan, and at lunch that day I told him about my trip to the Marlborough Gallery. The affable Mr. Dillon, for whom I have great respect, listened attentively, but I never heard anything more about it.

Hoving brought great numbers of people to the Museum. During his decade as director, attendance skyrocketed, as it did at other museums as well. He put on blockbuster exhibitions that brought in money and crowds. Of course, the merits of blockbusters are debatable—the shows are so crowded, it's difficult to view the art. I believe there will be fewer blockbuster shows in the future.

Hoving's successor, Philippe de Montebello, is in my opinion doing a fantastic job, as is William Luers, who is the second paid president of the Metropolitan Museum. Between the two of them, the Met runs beautifully.

METROPOLITAN HONORARY TRUSTEE

In January 1968, I received a letter that sent me not to seventh heaven but to eighth heaven. The Metropolitan Museum of Art had established a new category called "honorary trustee." I was invited to occupy one of these positions. I was tremendously happy and honored. It was the greatest event of my art life. I loved and respected the Met more than just about any place in the world.

Previously, the honorary trustees had been the mayor of New York City, the governor of the State, and the New York City parks commissioner, during the time they were in office. Arthur Houghton, a cousin of Alice Tully and president of the Met, set up a new form: lifetime trustees who were to be carefully selected for their service to the Metropolitan Museum and to art in general.

I was one of three people who, in January 1968, became the first permanent honorary trustees. The others were Professor Craig Smythe, head of the New York University Institute of Fine Arts, and Millard Meis, a great medieval art scholar at Princeton University. In May 1996, Kitty Carlisle Hart, former head of the New York State Commission on the Arts, a talented woman who has done a great deal for art in America, also became an honorary trustee.

At the time that I became an honorary trustee, it was alleged that there was some anti-Semitism at the Met. But Millard Meis was of Jewish lineage, as was I. Our appointments, I believe, demonstrated that by 1968, being Jewish was not much of a factor.

The Trustees of the Metropolitan gave me a bunch of cards that read "Roy Neuberger, Honorary Trustee." I have virtually the same access to go in and out of the Museum as employees have. I have been awarded three honorary degrees, but being an honorary trustee of the Met is much more important to me.

THE ART PENDULUM SWINGS

Beginning about 1958, the contemporary art scene in America began to change. The sale of contemporary art came to be dominated by extremely promotion-minded dealers. The collectors changed. So did the museum people. The whole world of art was changing. An artist could produce something that was very debatable as "art" and easily become famous. I felt that the art pendulum had swung too far, and I didn't want to be one to promote the movement.

By September 1958, the price of a Picasso had climbed so high that Victor Gans, the largest collector of Picasso in America, moved to American art. He wanted me to buy four Jasper Johns for $300 each. A quarter-century later, Sy Newhouse paid $17 million for a Jasper Johns. Johns was a very good artist, but that price tag was crazy.

About that time, I began buying ancient art and the works of Louis Eilshemius. I declared myself a free agent in 1958 and from then on bought whatever I liked, whether or not the artist was a living American. I was satisfied that I had accomplished what I had set out to do. I had personally helped support several hundred contemporary artists. Many people feel that I did exert some influence in getting collectors to consider buying art in support of living artists. I hope so.

A MUSEUM IN MY FUTURE

At a small Sunday-morning gathering in Washington, D. C., in 1966, my old mentor, a now frail Duncan Phillips, turned to me and said, "I feel that you are the only one whose taste resembles mine. I would very much like to see you have a museum in New York like mine in Washington." He died a few months later, but that seed was planted.

Shortly after seeing Phillips, I had lunch with President James Hester of New York University, who wanted to build an art museum. I was not particularly interested in taking part in his proposal, and ultimately the university opened the Grey Gallery rather than a new museum.

I think they did the right thing. There were too many museums in New York City, and this was not the place to add a Neuberger Museum.

Then along came Nelson Rockefeller.

Chapter 10

CREATING
THE NEUBERGER
MUSEUM OF ART

A MYSTERIOUS OFFER

In May 1965, as I was about to leave for a trip to Greece and Italy, I received an anonymous offer to buy my art collection for $5 million. In the years since, prices for art have skyrocketed, and the stock market has advanced about tenfold. But in the 1960s, $5 million was a fortune.

The offer was conveyed in a telephone call from a partner at Salomon Brothers. If a deal had been struck, Salomon Brothers would be paid a 5 percent commission by the anonymous purchaser. This Wall Street firm would collect $250,000, not on a securities transaction, but for the sale of an art collection.

At the time, I had no idea who was making the offer. Many years later, I learned from Charles Simon, a partner at Salomon Brothers, that the prospective buyer they were representing in their overtures was New York Governor Nelson Rockefeller.

I turned down the offer because I do not sell art.

To indicate how averse I am to selling art—quite the opposite of my feeling about stocks or bonds—I once received an offer from a great museum, the Chicago Art Institute, of $1 million in cash with a payment as well to the dealer, my friend Joan Washburn, for a rather small painting by Patrick Henry Bruce, a breakthrough artist who died in France in 1937. This painting of rather modest size had been previously owned by the Metropolitan Museum. A million dollars was very generous, but I turned it down.

MEETING WITH ROCKEFELLER

On a lovely Saturday in May 1967, Governor Rocke-feller invited Marie and me to lunch at Pocantico Hills, his spectacular estate in Westchester County with stunning views of the Hudson River.

Nelson's grandfather, the original John D. Rocke-feller, had built a house on this site in the first decade of the 20th century. Nelson's parents had a house at Pocantico Hills, as did his brother David and his brother Laurance. In fact, most of the family had houses on the estate. The family also had a nine-hole golf course, a croquet court, bowling alleys, and many other amenities.

Marie and I drove up from New York City with another couple, Lester and Joan Avnet. Lester was active in electronics, interested in art, and appeared to know Rockefeller fairly well; so he served as somewhat of a bridge between us.

We visited Nelson and his wife Happy from 11 A.M. until a little after 2 P.M. The first hour, we walked around the beautiful Pocantico Hills estate, viewing Nelson's great sculpture collection displayed on the grounds and admiring the brook he had built north of his home. The brook runs downhill to a Japanese house, itself a work of art. Then we had cocktails on the terrace. Nelson Rockefeller didn't drink much. He fondled a Dubonnet, and I had a martini. Lunch followed. Nelson and I talked privately during the third hour.

"Roy," he said, "I will build you a museum if you will donate your collection." When he said "I will build you a museum," he meant that the State of New York would build a museum.

He wanted the museum to be in Westchester County, at Purchase College of the State University of New York (SUNY). This campus was just being created. Plans had been drawn up, but construction had not yet begun.

Nelson envisioned Purchase College as the SUNY campus most devoted to the arts. In addition to an elegant art museum, the campus would have a complex of four theaters, including an opera house, and would have resources to teach ballet. The college would offer a total education, highlighting the best things in life—humanities, art, and culture.

"You give that collection," Nelson said. He felt that my collection was large and important enough so that he could convince the New York State Legislature to spend money on a distinguished building.

ART COLLECTOR JOSEPH HIRSHHORN

For the record, Rockefeller had also approached Joseph Hirshhorn, who had a diverse art collection, larger than mine and quite different. Hirshhorn and I were reputed to be the two largest collectors at the time, but we were very dissimilar in philosophy. He was interested in European art as well as American, and he was particularly strong in sculpture. He did not buy many paintings. A great Rodin sculpture, *The Burghers of Calais*, is at the Hirshhorn Sculpture Garden in Washington. Another casting of this superb sculpture is at the Metropolitan.

Joe Hirshhorn chose instead to accept the offer from President Lyndon Johnson to build a museum in Washington. You can see the controversial but beautiful museum there today—the Hirshhorn Sculpture Garden, built on the Mall, is part of the Smithsonian Museum complex. It was controversial because some people objected to taking land away from the Mall and using it for a private collection. Up until then, only great past presidents had been honored there. But President Johnson said that getting the Hirshhorn collection was a great coup. So the Hirshhorn Sculpture Garden is on the Mall, with Washington and Lincoln.

I was pleased to be sitting at Joe Hirshhorn's table in Washington at the opening of the Sculpture Garden in October 1974. Five months earlier, we had opened the Neuberger Museum—two openings in one year, just five months apart.

MY REPLY TO ROCKEFELLER

I liked what I heard from Governor Rockefeller, but I did not say yes on that first occasion. Less than two weeks later, I received a letter from him expressing great excitement about the project and inviting me for cocktails. He also invited SUNY Chancellor Samuel Gould and Abbott Kaplan, who was being imported from UCLA to be President of SUNY-Purchase College. We met at Nelson's house in Manhattan, on Fifth Avenue at East 62nd Street, and we consumed an indecent amount of caviar, smoked salmon, and other hors d'oeuvres.

At this second meeting, Governor Rockefeller said that he wanted me to assist in developing the new campus, to work as a volunteer to help the college become outstanding. I can't overstate how animated he was about this cultural and educational project and how much these things meant to him. His enthusiasm and his genuine and passionate love of art were contagious. Perhaps I was affected by his excitement and his natural feeling for education and culture when I accepted his offer in June 1967.

Rockefeller wanted SUNY-Purchase College to be the "jewel of the State University system." I'm not sure he should have said that because there are 63 other campuses vying for the honor. Then he made another statement that perhaps he shouldn't have. He said, "It is understood that we don't want any money from you." I remember that distinctly. I laughed a little.

ROCKEFELLER THE POLITICIAN

Nelson Rockefeller was a unique politician, one of the most vibrant people who ever lived. He loved humanity and art, and I respected him and liked him. Senator Barry Goldwater, however, thought he was a terrible man and said so at the Republican Convention in 1964. Goldwater became the Republican candidate for president that year and lost overwhelmingly to President Lyndon Johnson. In my opinion, Rockefeller was too liberal for the Republican Party. Of course, he may not have appeared that way to much of the public because he wasn't a liberal in every respect. I made a suggestion to him before the 1968 Republican Convention: "Nelson, why don't you become a Democrat? Then you could beat Mr. Nixon." He only smiled. He was a very strong Republican. His nephew Senator Jay Rockefeller of West Virginia is a strong Democrat.

I supported Nelson enthusiastically when he sought the Republican nomination for President in 1968, and I worked hard to get him nominated. As a member of his finance committee, I raised more money for him than anyone except the committee chairman, Jock Whitney.

One morning, following a finance committee meeting at Nelson's office on West 55th Street, he said to me, "Roy, today I am going to give you a ride to work." He was giving a speech at the subtreasury building in the Wall Street area. My office at the time was located downtown at 120 Broadway. We drove down in his car.

Wherever Nelson went in those days, he drew large crowds. When we got to lower Broadway the traffic was so heavy that we came to a standstill. Nelson got out of the car at Fulton Street and climbed aboard a double decker bus. That added some flair to his arrival at the subtreasury building a few blocks further south. While Nelson was making his entrance, I arrived at work in grand style in the Governor's limousine.

That same day, Nelson said, "Roy, I want you to come to the Republican convention in Miami." I told him, "I don't like Miami, particularly in August. I've never been to a convention, but I suspect that I won't like it." But Rockefeller never accepted no as an answer. He said, "Roy, you must come to the convention. I want you to be there. You are going to go there." And so I did.

The 1968 Republican Convention was disastrous. I stayed until almost the last moment, when the voting started. But I decided to fly out of Miami before the airport became too crowded with everyone else flying out. I arrived back at my apartment in New York at exactly midnight, in time to hear the end of the voting. Richard Nixon was the Republican presidential candidate and was elected in November.

I think it is interesting that, like Winston Churchill, the greatest man of the century in my opinion, Rockefeller was dyslexic in his early years. There is even a Winston School in New York for dyslexic children, named for Churchill. Rockefeller and Churchill are just two of many high-achieving adults who have suffered from dyslexia.

If Nelson had been successful in his quest for the presidency, elected in 1968 instead of Mr. Nixon, I believe United States history might have been much better. The history of the world might have been better. Rockefeller had a very good mind, and I believe that he would have been one of the great presidents.

BUILDING THE MUSEUM

I liked the idea of a Neuberger Museum of Art. After our second meeting, Nelson Rockefeller and I made a verbal agreement, including a decision that Philip Johnson would design the building. I was particularly pleased that an architect of Johnson's stature would design my museum.

The process proceeded slowly. No papers were signed until two years later. For someone who trades thousands of securities with the flick of a button, it was difficult waiting so long to execute an already-agreed-upon plan. The pace was much slower than the way I usually operate.

When we signed the agreement in the fall of 1969, the *New York Times* printed a picture of Nelson Rockefeller, my wife, myself, and Dr. Samuel Gould, the SUNY chancellor, looking at an Edward Hopper painting in my collection. We agreed that I would give most of my paintings to the museum. Of course, I couldn't give them what I had already given to other institutions. And it was also understood that the pieces displayed in my homes and office would remain there.

Philip Johnson designed a splendid building for the Neuberger Museum. I think even Johnson himself was surprised at how good it was. It was the first structure to be completed on the new Purchase College campus, in 1971, before there was a library or any usable classrooms—it *was* the Purchase College campus. For the first three years of SUNY-Purchase's existence, the museum building did not function as a museum. Instead, the museum basement, which is now a huge art storeroom, housed the growing Purchase library. The museum building also provided classrooms and work space for students of visual arts, music, and drama.

OPENING THE MUSEUM

By 1974, the campus had begun to take shape. Other buildings were completed and open to students. We could reclaim the building that was built for our museum. The Neuberger Museum of Art opened in May of that year with a marvelous show of paintings and sculptures that included works from my collection, some new acquisitions purchased by the Founding Friends of the Neuberger Museum, and some pieces from other collections.

Bryan Robertson, the first director of the Neuberger Museum, was responsible for my working with Henry Moore to negotiate the acquisition of a statue for the campus. I already knew Mr. Moore slightly from 1958 when I had purchased some of his small bronzes and a 1937 drawing.

The magnificent 18-foot-high, six-ton, Henry Moore bronze statue, which today serves as a visual focal point on the Purchase College campus, is there in part because of Henry Moore's generosity. On the occasion of our opening, he said he would let the museum have the sculpture if we would pay for the casting in Germany at a cost of $89,000. The casting turned out to be even more expensive than that, and Mr. Moore paid for it himself. The college paid the huge fee to put it in place. It is my hope that the Henry Moore bronze will attract additional modern sculpture to enhance the campus.

At the time of the Museum opening, we also showed a beautiful white marble statue by Isamu Noguchi from my collection. Noguchi was a friend of mine and one of the great sculptors of the century, though not quite the equal of Henry Moore. He loaned another large marble for our opening. After the show, he left it at the museum, and ultimately, before he died, he donated this second sculpture to the college.

Marble sculptures are particularly significant gifts because they are unique. There can be only one. A bronze sculpture is one of several castings. An artist usually makes somewhere between six and nine castings of an important bronze piece. So even the most wonderful bronze is not unique.

And Noguchi made the donation even though the tax deductibility was negligible. According to the law, he could write off only the cost of the marble and not the value of the art. The laws governing gifts from artists are unaccommodating, to put it mildly. I suspect this is the result of an incident that occurred around the same time. It involved the director of the Guggenheim Museum—she was a painter who donated some of her work to the Museum at an exceedingly overvalued worth. I would guess that Congress found this unacceptable and, as a result, passed a rather harsh law.

We were very fortunate in securing the services of Alexander Lieberman to create a cover for the opening show's catalog. Lieberman was a Renaissance man—a sculptor, painter, and photographer whose abilities were great in every direction. He was regarded as an extremely fine professional photographer, and his gigantic sculptures are respected by many. He was also well known as a business man, as the art director of Vogue magazine, and as the editorial director of all the Conde Nast magazines.

Lieberman photographed me in front of the Jackson Pollock, next to an ancient Chinese sculpture. He took more than 100 photographs before he was satisfied that he had one for the catalog cover. Inside the catalog, Governor Nelson Rockefeller wrote:

"The opening of the Neuberger Museum, in this imaginative building, housing this important collection, on this new campus, magnifies beyond measure the potential of each of these works of art to reach people, to give pleasure, and to lift the human spirit.

"Though the Neuberger Museum will serve the entire community, the fact that it is part of a college campus is particularly fortunate . . . thousands of people, now and for generations to come, will become more sensitized to beauty and to the world around them through the art surrounding them in the Neuberger Museum."

I like to think that Nelson was right.

THE PURCHASE COLLEGE FOUNDATION

At Rockefeller's urging, I became involved in the development of the Purchase College campus. After Nelson died in 1979, I recognized that it was fortunate that I had taken a large role in shaping the direction of the college. I could see the way the wind was blowing: we were headed for some tough financial times.

There was no fund-raising arm of the college until I helped create the Purchase College Foundation, which acts like a board of trustees. The State University doesn't have trustees for each campus, but we performed that function at Purchase. I was chairman of the Foundation from 1974 to 1988 when I reached the age of 85. After my 85th birthday, I resigned from the chairmanship and from the board.

The Foundation was somewhat neglected by Abbott Kaplan, the first president of Purchase College. Sheldon Grebstein, his successor for about 10 years, did a good job in the development of the campus and of the Purchase College Foundation. The current president, Bill Lacy, understands the importance of fund-raising for an educational institution and is very supportive of it.

Pepsico has its headquarters across the road from the Purchase College campus and has been extremely helpful in supporting performing arts programs at the college. When Don Kendall was CEO of Pepsico, he was particularly generous in providing grants.

By the end of 1996, the Neuberger Museum endowment in the Purchase College Foundation was worth about $6.6 million. I added a $5 million challenge grant, with the first million given in December 1996. The museum needs to raise this considerable sum because of current inadequacies in funding by the state and federal governments.

FUNDING THE MUSEUM

The conditions facing nonprofit cultural institutions all over the country have changed a great deal in the past 25 years. It has been incumbent upon private capital, both individuals and corporations, to put up the money that is no longer forthcoming from government. This shift has come at a time when the level of cultural activity has greatly increased. The Neuberger Museum of Art, like others, has to raise money from private sources for acquisition, educational outreach, exhibits, special programs, and all the other things a lively museum on a college campus should be undertaking.

Because we loan paintings all over the world, we are visible—which helps raise money. We were fortunate in having the backing of the Founding Friends of the Neuberger Museum, formed in 1972, to help launch the museum. This wonderful group of supporters then metamorphosed into a permanent Friends of the Neuberger Museum, who do an extraordinary job of supporting the activities of the museum.

The museum's collection of ancient art began with a gift from Nelson Rockefeller of 17 ancient Greek vases that had belonged to his aunt Lucy Aldrich. Rockefeller had written me a letter saying that he was going to give money to the Neuberger Museum, but he never did. We received the vases and a few other minor pieces, but no money. In 1996, we displayed these vases along with my collection of ancient art. It was considered a very fine show.

For more than 20 years, the museum has served well as a place for permanent exhibits and special shows put together by a terrific staff. I visit every few weeks. My driver, Jimmy McCloud, likes to take me there because nearby, on property I own, there's a brook with good fishing.

Our insightful museum director, Lucinda Gedeon, and I talk every day. She and her husband, a fine man and an excellent artist, live in a house that I bought for the use of the museum director, just five minutes from the Museum.

CELEBRATING THE ROCKEFELLERS

On Thursday, September 26, 1996, 29 years after my first visit, I once again roamed the spectacular grounds of the Pocantico Hills estate and sat on the same terrace of the Rockefeller house where Marie and I had first lunched with Nelson and Happy Rockefeller. This time I was invited by Happy Rockefeller and Laurance and Mary Rockefeller to meet with about 30 people in the family playhouse to put finishing touches on plans for a day honoring Nelson on the 25th anniversary of the creation of Purchase College. Mary Rockefeller, who has since died, was a hostess of this event.

A symposium held on campus three days later, a clear, crisp autumn Sunday, was moderated by the popular public television host Charlie Rose. The only woman on the panel was the charming Kitty Carlisle Hart, who for 20 years served as New York State Cultural Affairs Commissioner. I was pleased to have this opportunity to resume my acquaintance with her.

We had originally met at a small dinner party on the occasion of a John Rockefeller gift of Asian art to Asia House. Today Asia House occupies a large building at Park Avenue and East 70th Street. At the time that I met Kitty Carlisle Hart at dinner, it was a small museum located on East 64th Street near Lexington Avenue.

There were several small dinner parties that night before we gathered at Asia House to celebrate the John Rockefeller gift. Marie and I were invited to the home of a dealer named Elsworth who sold a considerable amount of Asian art to John Rockefeller. Elsworth was a bachelor who lived in a beautiful private house filled with magnificent Asian art. On this occasion, Kitty Carlisle Hart was his hostess. Other guests were the director of the Cleveland Art Museum and a scholar in Asian art, Sherman Lee, and his wife, and John and Blanchette Rockefeller. It was a dinner party of eight.

I was rather astonished to be included at a dinner for the donor and honoree of the evening and two outstanding Asian art experts because I had only three pieces of ancient Asian art. One is the great Chinese piece that was in the photograph for the cover of the catalog of the opening show at the Neuberger Museum of Art.

After dinner, we walked a block or so to Asia House for the ceremony.

Not long afterward, John Rockefeller came to see me in my office to discuss the possibility of Asia House moving to 70th Street. I advised that they stay where they were. I told him that it was a very popular place. But Rockefellers don't stay put. They build and move.

The Purchase College panel took up aspects of Nelson Rockefeller's life relating to politics, education, and art, including the influence of his mother. More than 1,200 people attended, including Nelson's widow Happy Rockefeller and other members of the Rockefeller family. It was followed by a reception at the Neuberger Museum of Art where Happy's son Mark and I were the speakers, introduced by Bill Lacy, President of the College.

I mentioned that former New York City Mayor John Lindsay had converted from being a Republican to a Democrat, and I recalled the advice I had given to Nelson years ago, that he do the same.

At the end of the day, I gave Kitty Carlisle Hart a ride home to her apartment in Manhattan just a few blocks from where I live. She had a heavy bag because she was coming from a singing engagement on Long Island. She said that although she didn't need the money, she had made some by singing, something she hadn't done in a while. She is really a terrific lady. It turned out she and I knew Nelson Rockefeller better than anyone else at the symposium, except for his relatives. Following the Purchase College day, I was fortunate enough to have Kitty as a dinner guest several times.

A WISE INVESTMENT

I have already given about 800 works of art to the Neuberger Museum of Art. I plan to give many more. The museum continues to acquire other works, proceeding along the path I charted many years ago, broadening its horizon to include fine pieces from many periods in history.

In the beginning, I collected art for a purpose—to help support living artists. Now I am simply a lover of art. I plan to give to the museum my collection of ancient art, which dates back to before the birth of Christ.

To see the wonderful paintings I collected studied by students and art lovers from all over the world is one of my greatest joys. Working with Nelson Rockefeller and Philip Johnson to get the museum going was one of the smartest investments of my life.

Chapter 11

TEN PRINCIPLES OF SUCCESSFUL INVESTING

The stock market is like a large, treacherous ocean, with tides moving in and out. Market waves are less frequent than the ocean's, but they are more erratic. Even the strongest swimmer must carefully time advances and retreats. Like swimming in the ocean, investing in the market is not for everyone. I would advise most investors to work with experienced professionals. It is well worth paying a modest fee for the service. Pursue your own passions, and leave the bulk of the investing to a professional.

If you have substantial capital, get a qualified investment counselor, someone whom you can trust and who understands your needs. You can also delegate effectively by investing in no-load mutual funds.

Some smaller investors have done quite well over a period of years, competing with the professionals in their own right. They've succeeded through careful analysis of a company prior to purchasing its stock.

One of the best of these investors was an insurance man named Jack Sloan. He did better than 99 percent of the Wall Street professionals. He didn't do much trading, but he was the wisest investor I ever met.

Small investors who get into trouble, I think, are those who try to get rich quick. They are in and out of the market in a flash and don't take the time to learn. That's a dangerous game.

The market of the 1990s is very speculative—with a lot of volatility. Getting into the market is tempting when you read about fortunes made on Wall Street. But you should realize that the professionals who make enormous gains are not lottery winners. In most cases, they do not play long odds—they are experts who know what they're doing.

Among the tens of millions of people and institutions who buy and sell each day, more of them are amateurs today than ever before. If you are one of them, and if I haven't succeeded in scaring you off or convinced you to get help from the professionals, I want to give you the best advice I can.

From the hundreds of lessons that have guided me, I have culled 10 important principles that have served me well for nearly seven decades of successful and enjoyable investing and trading.

In 68 years of buying and selling securities, I have used these tools to my advantage. I hope they will help you.

1. KNOW THYSELF

In the modern economy, we no longer heed Polonius's advice to his son Laertes: "Neither a borrower nor a lender be." But another part of the father's advice is timelier than ever: "This above all, to thine own self be true."

Your personal strengths will help determine your success as an investor. Before you begin studying companies for investment, study yourself.

I think I have the right personality for Wall Street. When I was a buyer at B. Altman, I discovered that I had an aptitude for trading. There, we traded inventory for cash and cash for inventory. For me, trading has always been more instinctive than long-term investing, which requires enormous patience. Trading involves quick decisions. After reviewing some of the factors discussed here, you will be in a better position to decide if you are the right kind of person to enter the market.

Examine your own temperament. Are you by nature very speculative? Or are you uncomfortable taking risks? Be 100 percent honest with yourself in answering this question. You must be able to make calm judgments. *Calm* does not mean *slow*. It means careful decisions based on solid knowledge. Sometimes a move must be made fast. Usually, if you have done your homework, quick decision making won't be a problem.

If you feel you have made a mistake, get out fast. The stock market is not like real estate, where you have to wait a long time for your judgment to be ratified. One difference between real estate and the stock market is that in the market you can move around like a jack rabbit.

You need a high level of energy. You need to be quick with figures. And, most of all, you need common sense.

You have to be intensely interested in what you are doing. My primary interest is not money. But I don't like to lose. I like to win.

Success in investing is based on applying knowledge and experience. It is a good idea to specialize and to invest in areas in which you already have specific knowledge. If you know nothing about an area and haven't studied the companies and the sector, stay away from it.

I haven't put a lot of money into foreign investments because I don't know a darn thing about them. I hardly ever make trades in foreign securities. For the most part, I'm a local investor. I do my international investing through local companies. Most of the major companies in which I invest have interests all over the globe. IBM, for instance, makes at least half of its profits overseas.

We have an international fund at Neuberger & Berman. I own some of it for my family. I really should increase my holding, but I pay much more attention to the sectors in which I am most experienced. For instance, I am experienced at hedging—being "short" some stocks and "long" others at the same time—but I do not recommend this to others. One has to have a stubborn, perverse, and patient temperament.

Temperament also plays an important role in how one uses the market's modern techniques, such as index funds; futures based on the Standard & Poor's 500 and other stock indexes; and put and call options, which are used to a far greater degree than they were 20 or 30 years ago. Personally, I don't care for options, but sometimes I use futures in commodities. I don't recommend it for individual investors.

Before becoming an active investor, it is also important to be sure that you are in good physical and mental condition. Don't underestimate the importance of good health as it pertains to smart decision making.

2. STUDY THE GREAT INVESTORS

Even the most successful investors have had a hard time in this end-of-the-century market. I speak to many of them, and only a handful found 1996 easy to read, despite the fact that it was a year of continual advancement.

Many of the outstanding investors of the past would have a difficult time in the current market. Nonetheless, lessons learned from their careers can be applied to the market at any time, even in times as crazy as the 1990s.

There are two broad theories of investing on Wall Street: growth and value. At Neuberger&Berman, we take what we call a value approach to securities. This means that we buy securities that sell at a reasonable multiple of earnings. In olden days, this usually meant 10 times earnings. But times have changed: I take into consideration the amount of growth. If the growth is 30 percent, I am willing to pay 20 x earnings. If the growth is 20 percent, I will pay 15 x earnings. But in general I want to buy stocks at a multiple lower than the growth by a considerable margin.

For instance, Coca-Cola grows at 10 to 15 percent— averaging 12 percent a year. It has sold for as high as 37 x earnings. I wouldn't think of buying it. Yet Warren Buffett, perhaps the most successful investor in the world, has lots of it. It is his biggest position.

I have been short on Coca-Cola for a long time. I'm addicted to drinking it and addicted to thinking it is an overvalued company. It produces an unhealthful product. It's funny how well vices can do. Look what Philip Morris has done with cigarettes. No question about it, you can make money investing in vice. Gambling stocks can be very successful, too.

A stock I've preferred is Johnson & Johnson, the huge health-care-product company. I have been heavily long on Johnson & Johnson. I was impressed by its fast growth—net sales, net income, and global scope. I thought its multiple was reasonable.

Our firm's reputation is based on the fact that we buy what we think are good values, and we hope that they will go up in value. In 1995, the *Wall Street Journal* rated the Guardian Fund as number one for five years in *value investing*. But a lot of people make just as much money by buying overpriced stocks that seem to go higher and higher.

Looking at the careers of great investors, it is clear that there are many different, often contradictory, ways to succeed:

T. Rowe Price succeeded by appreciating the importance of the growth of new industries. Ben Graham did it by understanding basic values. Warren Buffett did it by elaborating on the lessons he learned from Ben Graham, his teacher at Columbia University. George Soros did it by relating a thoughtful philosophy to international finance. Jimmy Rogers did it by discovering defense industry stocks and by passing along ideas and analyses to his boss, George Soros. Each has been highly successful in his own way.

Warren Buffett and Ben Graham

Warren Buffett is a "one decision" man. He buys them and holds them. He is, I believe, the greatest investor around. He emphasizes that he owes everything to Ben Graham, whom I knew well. But Buffett knows more than Ben Graham did.

When I met Buffett some years ago at the opening of a Degas show at the Tisch galleries, I told him, "I know how important Ben Graham was to you. You have far exceeded his ability."

I believe in Ben Graham's theories. I read his landmark book *Security Analysis* a long time ago. But unlike Graham, I do not believe that if a stock goes up, say, 50 percent, and gets fully priced, you should necessarily sell it.

I made a proposition to Ben Graham in 1957 during

lunch at the Bankers Club. At the time, I was the largest stockholder in Tri-Continental (for my firm, my clients, the Guardian Mutual Fund, and myself). I held so much of the stock because it was such a good value—a blue-chip stock you could buy at a 33 percent discount from asset value on the Exchange. Tri-Continental was the largest investment trust on the Exchange, run by Seligman, a fine conservative firm.

"If we worked to take over the management of Tri-Continental," I told Ben Graham, "and we told the world that Ben Graham would be the president, we would have a tremendously popular billion-dollar fund."

Ben Graham said, "Roy, you are perfectly right; we could gain control. But I have lost interest in the whole matter, and in a few years I am going to retire." That was the end of that.

Graham didn't make his big money on the rules he propounded. He did it by buying into the shares of GEICO (Government Employees Insurance Company) in 1948. The public thought that GEICO had extra safety because of the word *government*. But it had nothing to do with the government, though it originally insured preferred-risk drivers, many of them government employees.

When GEICO became a billion-dollar firm, Ben Graham's shares were worth millions. His Columbia student, Warren Buffett, who had invested $10,000 in GEICO and sold at a 50 percent profit, purchased the company a quarter-century later and made a fortune. Buffett saved the company from bankruptcy. Earlier, the stock had gone from over 100 to under 1. Many people who followed Graham, even after he was dead, thought they were rich when, in fact, they weren't.

In May 1996, an article in *Forbes* magazine contended that Warren Buffett is reaching the peak of his career and may start sliding. I have no idea if that is true, but if it is, it doesn't mean that Mr. Buffett will ever be poor. Even brilliant people top out—the greatest mountain has two sides.

Peter Lynch

I consider Warren Buffett and Peter Lynch to be the two greatest investors in modern history. They, along with George Soros, are the investors to whom I would apply the word *genius*.

If I had to pick one impeccable, overall investor, it would have to be Peter Lynch. He is number one in character. He did a Herculean job on Wall Street and knew when to quit to focus on his family. I have enormous respect for him.

Peter Lynch took the Magellan Fund from low figures to $14 billion. He owned 1,500 stocks, understood them all, and made a much greater profit than any other fund. But in 1990, he decided that he was not spending enough time with his family. He thought that his work schedule would eventually wreck him, so he announced his retirement. He didn't retire completely, though. He is an important executive in Fidelity Investments and a best-selling investment author.

George Soros

There are a lot of good traders, and many more bad ones. Only a handful can be called "great traders." George Soros is one of the great traders. He is a superb international investor, handling billions and billions in futures and currencies, in addition to stocks and bonds. Some of his choices may not be the safest places to put money. They are much more speculative than one thought 50 years ago. But I have great confidence in Mr. Soros as a brilliant mind.

I believe that Mr. Soros is an outstanding human being as well. He is exceptionally generous. He gives away hundreds of millions of dollars through foundations in 25 countries, including those of Eastern Europe and the former Soviet Union. He has made major contributions to education, culture, science, and human rights. He is unmatched by his peers.

I went to his home when he hosted a charity event, an unusual thing for him to do because he has supported a number of charities over the years very quietly. More recently, in December 1996, he did attract public attention with his plan to earmark half of his annual giving, which is in the hundreds of millions, to critical issues in the United States, such as the improvement of education and the protection of the rights of legal immigrants.

Jimmy Rogers

Soros's onetime assistant, Jimmy Rogers, is regarded as something of a Wall Street character. I was told in 1996 that Jimmy appeared on CNBC and called me his mentor.

Jimmy Rogers came up from the South. He was young and obviously very bright. For nine months in 1970, he was my assistant. I developed such confidence in him that I gave him 15 percent of Guardian Mutual

Fund to invest. Now he is a professor frequently on television sharing his expertise.

Jimmy is very brainy. He doesn't do what everyone else does. He left me suddenly to join George Soros as his assistant, and he soon became second in command. During the time Jimmy was with Soros, they made a lot of money by going short on Avon products. I too was very bearish on Avon. I thought it was ridiculously over-priced.

When Jimmy Rogers left Mr. Soros, he was paid $14 million dollars. His career since has included teaching at Columbia, appearing on TV, motor cycling, and becoming knowledgeable about the securities markets in many, many countries. He has become an authority on international investments.

Michael Steinhardt

George Soros established the largest of the hedge fund firms. Michael Steinhardt, another of the great hedgers, was not far behind. Steinhardt is a brilliant, charming man (much younger than I) who had an office in the same building as Neuberger&Berman and a house near mine in Westchester County. He has been an extremely successful manager of a large hedge fund and, I understand, a tough boss.

In 1995, Steinhardt got fed up with the market. He sold every long, covered every short, and went out of the business 100 percent, saying that he had enough money and wanted to pursue other interests. But like me, he still comes to the office and trades for himself from his own considerable resources.

He bought my real estate partner's house in northern Westchester and a lot of property right on the Croton Reservoir near Bedford. My house has a long vista overlooking the reservoir; his property goes right to the shore. One house on his property, with a gigantic swimming pool, once belonged to Theodore Dreiser, the early-20th-century novelist who wrote *An American Tragedy.*

Steinhardt imported many animals and developed a virtual zoo on his property. He fixed up everything for the animals and created a sort of African preserve.

Robert Wilson

Bob Wilson was fantastic. He was a friendly, bright man, and in many ways a much better trader than I am. He, too, made a fortune and quit to devote his life to more cultural areas.

Wilson was one of the best speculators in Wall Street history. He invested only for himself, for his own account, clearing through Neuberger&Berman and another firm. He was brilliant on both sides of the market, long and short.

When Bob Wilson quit, he turned his money over to 27 different professionals. Each invests it differently.

Joseph Kennedy

I would classify Joseph Kennedy, the father of President John F. Kennedy and Senators Robert and Edward Kennedy, as a great speculator. I learned this about him during my first months on Wall Street when I wrote out many of his transactions. And I watched him operate in the market in later years. He had many accounts with a number of different brokers.

When President Roosevelt nominated Joe Kennedy to be the first head of the Securities and Exchange Commission, I was astounded. But Mr. Kennedy's good behavior in that position showed me that you can never really be sure that you understand another person.

Michael Milken

I know very little about the rules that Michael Milken broke because I don't play in the junk bond market. I don't know him, I had no trades with him. He invented what are called "junk bonds," which merely means that the interest rate was substantially higher than the AAA and AA bonds of American Telephone & Telegraph and the older concerns. New firms come up and their credit rating is dubious at first.

Milken created a new market. He was so astute that he got a $650 million check from his firm for one year's services. He was as brilliant as Buffett, only his direction was different. From everything I have read and heard about him, I believe that he is a decent man.

I don't have the same feeling, however, about many other famous speculators who milk companies for the benefit of number one. They may be operating legally (some of the time) but their sense of morality is quite different from my own.

3. BEWARE OF THE SHEEP MARKET

My advice is to *learn* from the great investors—not *follow* them. You can benefit from their mistakes and successes, and you can *adapt* what fits your temperament and circumstances. Your resources and your needs are bound to be different from anyone you may want to emulate.

There is a pervasive trend, particularly strong in the late 1990s, that has investors blindly following the lead of others, mostly strangers. If there is a positive or negative statement from one analyst knowledgeable about certain securities or if an opinion is given by one key player, investors follow that person, whom they probably don't even know. And the market responds violently.

This is a momentary blip. It doesn't continue for a week. It just happens that day. One individual comments on a stock, and it moves up or down 10 percent. That could not be called a real bull market or bear market.

I call it a "sheep market." Sometimes the lambs are led to slaughter. Sometimes they merely get fleeced. Other times they are lucky and escape with their lives and their wool.

The sheep market is a little bit like the fashion industry. When a great couturier makes a new style of dress or suit, the minor designers copy it. If the hem lines on a dress go up or down, millions of people follow the fashion. That is a sheep market.

The sheep market adds to the problems in the 1990s market. You could never be absolutely sure of the market, but today uncertainty is greater than ever before. I am nervous about a market that, by and large, has gone up for two decades. Along the way, when it drops more than 100 points in a day, you know it's a sheep market. There are millions of amateurs playing the market, moving into mutual funds like never before, following each other; and so the market follows them.

Today's market needs Dr. Freud to put it on a couch and analyze it. It is a very neurotic market, motivated by far different factors than it used to be.

Don't underestimate the importance of psychology in the stock market. When people buy, they are more anxious to buy than the seller is to sell, and vice versa. Many factors go into the buy or sell decision besides economic statistics or security analysis. A bad buy or sell decision may be made merely because of a headache.

In the sheep market, people try to guess what the crowd will do, believing they can be swept along in a favorable current. That can be dangerous. The crowd may be very late in acting. Suppose it's an institutional crowd. Sometimes they overinfluence each other and are the victims of their own habits.

Sheep investors are very susceptible to suggestion. It is much better to do your own research and choose stocks on their merit than it is to take tips that you really can't substantiate.

4. KEEP A LONG-TERM PERSPECTIVE

A sizable part of the Wall Street community appears to be obsessed with finding out what is happening to corporate earnings from minute to minute. The greatest game among a number of research firms today seems to be to determine next quarter's earnings before someone else does.

This focus on short-term earnings ignores the significance of longer trends. Corporations often must make expenditures, with an effect on current earnings, to build for the future. If the goal of showing immediate gains in earnings becomes dominant, it can be detrimental to a company's future.

Gains in earnings should be the result of long-term strategies, proper management, and good exploitation of opportunities. If these things fall in place, short-term earnings shouldn't always be a major factor.

Another problem with microanalysis is the fallout when a very popular company underperforms in a quarter. Then surprise in the marketplace causes the stock price drop.

Keeping a long-term perspective in investing will keep you from being diverted by fads. There have always been fads on Wall Street, from the Stutz Bearcat autos of the 1920s to the bowling stocks of the late 1950s. People seemed to believe that every American man, woman, and child would become a bowler. But like the hula hoop, this fad came to an end. Those who bought early prospered; those who bought late at very high multiples were taken to the alleys.

Conglomerates became a fad in the 1960s when reported earnings were often boosted by some athletic bookkeeping. The criteria for purchase of any substantial amount of stock should remain on solid grounds that stand the test of time: (1) a good product; (2) a necessary product; (3) honest, effective management; and (4) honest reporting.

An investment can always be affected by a bit of luck, but fads come and go. Watch the big trends on Wall Street over a long period of time. You will find that the market generally seems to have long waves of advances lasting about two years. It also has waves of declines lasting a shorter period, perhaps one-half the period of the upswing. During the decline, there is extreme irregularity in most individual securities, affording institutions and individuals great opportunities for enhancement of wealth.

I am a great fan of keeping charts. They tell you a lot in a hurry about a company or a trend or how your investments are doing. Even in the computer age, it helps if you chart your own progress, as my partner Howard Lipman, the artist and floor trader, and I began to do back in 1930.

I have a chart that shows that in the 20th century we have had 26 bear markets and 27 bull markets. From 1974 (and particularly the summer of 1982) into mid-1997, we have had the most prolonged bull market in my lifetime. Unlike the current bull market, the two other major bull markets (1921–1929 and 1950–1972) were both punctuated by counter moves down against the trend.

Some market dips are significant, most are not. On Friday, March 8, 1996, the market went down by 170 points and made headlines. At the moment it seemed serious, but it was just a 3 percent correction—not historically important. Over the years, the market has dipped more than 3 percent many times.

In a real bear market, stocks decline 20 percent or more. During the 1987 panic, the market went down 508 points, or 22.6 percent in one day, worse than any one day in 1929. But the 1987 panic was not followed by a bear market. There was no economic justification for it. The market had gone up too fast for the circumstances, an extreme movement upward. The bond yield at the time was high and very competitive with the stock market. One of my charts shows the existence of a *real* bear market in 1973 and 1974 when the market went down about 45 percent.

During the period from 1929 to 1932, the loss was 89 percent. That was a *grizzly* bear market. It was followed by the worst Depression in modern times, more significant than the Panic of 1929 that caused the loss of entire fortunes in a moment. The significance of the Depression was the widespread, lasting economic dislocation of millions of people.

The 1929 market was prophetic—it signaled the dire circumstances ahead for the economy. We went very quickly into a world Depression that was not fully corrected in America until the 1940s and World War II. That is our perspective now, a long-term retroactive perspective. At the time, some of us were not surprised. Nonetheless, during the Depression there was a considerable bull market from 1932 to 1933 and then again in 1937.

Panics are caused by extremes—the correction of the extremes is the panic. Luckily, true panics don't happen often. The period from January 1973 to October 1974 was a major bear market rather than a panic because it was spread over a year and three-quarters. Panics tend to be more compressed and sensational.

To anticipate long-term movement, watch your charts. Study the past. Become your own historian.

5. GET IN AND OUT IN TIME

When is it a good time to get into the market—to buy? And when is it a good time to get out and stay out—to sell?

Timing may not be everything, but it is a lot. What looks like the best long-term investment can be terrible if you buy at the wrong time. And sometimes you can make money in highly speculative stocks by buying at the right moment. The very best securities analysts can do well without following market trends, but it's a lot easier to work with the trends.

A speculator or investor is often successful because he or she is willing to commit large sums on the buy side when the market is weak, getting a lot of securities for the money. On the opposite side, the investor creates eventual buying power by having the guts—the common sense—to sell in the strong markets, liquidating comparatively few securities for high prices. That's a simple principle.

Correct timing is partly intuitive, partly contrary. Timing requires independence in thinking. Uptrends can occur during business-cycle downtrends, and declines can come in periods of full prosperity.

How important is intuition? The great economist Paul Samuelson observed that the stock market forecast "eight of the last three recessions." True enough, and intuition then becomes temporarily as important as knowledge of analytical securities.

Timing is delicate, sometimes exquisitely so. To go short on the right stock at the wrong time (on the way up) may be horrendously expensive. Ask those who went short on Litton, TelePrompTer, Levitz Furniture, Memorex, and many others—rightly but too soon. I knew a man who lost everything selling short in the summer of 1929, at the height of the bull market. He didn't have the reserves to hold out until autumn.

Bull markets tend to be longer than bear markets. A rise in prices tends to be slower or more erratic than a decline in prices. Bear markets tend to be shorter, more severe, more intense. But the market does have certain fairly consistent habits. Rarely do the market and business rise concurrently for more than six months. Rarely do they decline for more than six months.

In a bull market, it is advisable to restrain one's greed. There is an old Wall Street saying: "The bulls make money, the bears make money. But what happens to the pigs?" You can't make 101 percent. You shouldn't even strive to make 100 percent. Your goal should be 66 $^2/_3$ percent of a big move. Get out and then reinvest in something that has been newly studied.

Remember how Richard Whitney watched his stocks decline in 1929 until he was wiped out? He failed to follow the 10 percent rule: *If the stock is on the way down, take your loss at the 10 percent level.* This rule has helped me many times. Using the money elsewhere will usually be more fruitful than maintaining a mistaken position.

I have often seen investors stubbornly stick to a position, increase the potential loss, and wait many years to break even in the stock.

Another kind of investor, after showing paper losses and then having the opportunity to break even, eagerly gets out without trying to reappraise the current situation. Nine times out of ten, the security was then a *buy* rather than a *sell*.

The lesson one learns from such situations is that the market does not know about these individual transactions. There is no magic to the price *you* paid for a security. One must often learn the hard way the market's antics of evaluation and reevaluation. It is not just amateurs who fail to appreciate this. Many investment counselors believe in long-term investments in a common stock portfolio. They stay too long with a stock. I think that when securities have climbed well above their value, they must be sold, whether they are being held in pension funds for the benefit of government employees or teachers or for anyone else. For example, early in the 1970s I thought Xerox was overpriced. It was selling at 77 times earnings. Like every investor, I can be wrong, but I was right about that. In 1973 it crashed.

When a particular security starts to sell above a reasonable intrinsic value, your only problem in selling is taxes. People are always trying to avoid taxes. That's a big mistake. Pay them.

Take your profits even though the stock price is short of the top of the market. Bernard Baruch was an investor with terrific timing. His philosophy was to do well by not being greedy. He never attempted to get a top or a bottom. He bought when things were weak and sold when they were strong. He was an advocate of buying a bit too soon and selling a bit too soon. Our firm was fortunate enough to have him as a client in the last years of his life.

There is a Wall Street myth that if you hold a stock long enough, you will win. Overall, this is true, but it can't be applied to individual companies. Companies die out. In the 19th century, Erie Canal securities were a great investment.

In late 1996, IBM was the strongest stock on the board. Sometime in the future the computer business will slow down and be replaced by a newer development. I can envisage a time when computers will be eliminated just like the Erie Canal.

At this point in history, common stocks are the greatest form of investment. At another point, the same could be said of real estate. One has to be a student of change. Everything changes. I just don't believe you can have confidence in any industry for an infinite length of time.

6. ANALYZE THE COMPANIES CLOSELY

Study the company's management, the leaders, their track records, and their goals. Check the company's real assets—the value of the plant and equipment—and the cash behind each share, a concept of great concern early in the century but almost forgotten later on.

Today, with the affluent-society concept fading and the energy supply no longer boundless, companies with extra oil and gas reserves, real estate, unused coal and copper mines, great stands of forests, and other assets are again being given a substantial plus in appraising a stock's worth. And why not? Tangibles such as antique furniture, ancient and modern art, and real estate have undergone enormous price appreciation. If a company owns a lot of real property, that is a reason to own the stock. But these assets should be connected with the company's earning power and, therefore, tied into its ultimate worth.

Dividends are an important plus. If the company's dividend is safe, it helps put a floor on the price. Check into the company's payout policy. If it pays out 90 percent of its earnings, beware—it's usually a danger signal of a dividend cut ahead. If a company is paying out as little as 10 percent, that is also a warning. The average company pays out 40 to 60 percent of earnings as dividends. Most utility companies are more generous.

Many institutional investors have paid too little attention to the actual dividends paid out. Paradoxically, individual investors concerned with maximizing their income often make the size of the dividend too important a consideration.

For years the big growth stocks zoomed while paying 2 percent. On the other hand, utility stocks had a hard time after the early 1960s, even though the dividends may have been 4 percent back then and later doubled.

What is a "growth stock"? One intelligent growth-stock adherent thinks it means a company discovered in an early stage of its potential. But often the label stays with the company after it has become mature. The growth has slowed, but people or institutions continue to buy it because their imagination doesn't go beyond the obvious.

There is no magic to the phrase "growth stock." The word *growth* describes what we are all trying to do. Long before the phrase became popular, investors and speculators were trying to foresee which companies were going to fare well in earnings, gross business, and reputation in the future. Everyone hopes to unearth a company that produces a new product that will be commonly used. The trick is to discover those companies before you have to pay too high a price for them.

Sometimes, after a price decline, a company needs to be rediscovered. Many stocks that were popular and sold at high multiples in the late 1960s and early 1970s later came down drastically. Sometimes there was no problem with the company; the price of the stock was just too high. Several of those stocks became attractive again. They were companies that had stood the test of time. They were much better than the average big company, and their growth rates were more sustained.

In the 1920s, a brilliant and important book by Edgar Smith, *Common Stocks for Long-Term Investment*, became a prime market influence. It was still popular in the fall of 1929, but most people read it too late. Mr. Smith advocated the benefit to corporate growth of the application of retained earnings and depreciation. Thus capital appreciates. The book may have been influential in changing accepted multiples of 10 x earnings to higher multiples of 20 to 30 x earnings.

People have often paid too much for assumed persistent growth, only to discover that a general economic decline, an act of war, or a series of government controls changed either the appraisal of the growth rate or the growth rate itself.

Rarely can securities be valued correctly at over 15 x earnings because rarely is there any clear prospect that a company's earnings will grow sufficiently in the future to make it worth that price. We know that there are exceptions, but they account for perhaps 1 percent of the cases. So the odds are against you when you pay a very high multiple.

A multiple of between 10 and 15 on an outstanding company is acceptable to me, even if there are many stocks selling between 6 and 10 x earnings. There may be acceptable values in both groups.

You should always be summing up the total market value of a company. You can get a better grasp on values that way.

In the late 1970s, IBM was selling at $40 billion. At that time the total corporate wealth of the United States was estimated at $900 billion, so IBM's $40 billion was a big figure. But IBM was a very special company. On the other hand, in 1961, when IBM was much smaller, the company was selling in the market for $16 billion, which worked out to 80 x earnings, much too high. The following year the price dropped by 50 percent.

In 1972, Avon Products was selling in the market for $8 billion while it was earning about $125 million, or 64 x earnings. That also turned out to be much too high. In the early 1970s, Avon was my principal bear, a judgment that I was happy to share with Jimmy Rogers. I was short on Avon for myself, not for my institutions. I thought it was terribly overpriced. When the bear market finally developed, the stock collapsed down to one-tenth of what it had been.

I had lost money on Avon for a while. I had to have patience. It paid off.

7. DON'T FALL IN LOVE

One should fall in love with ideas, with people, or with idealism based on the possibilities that exist in this adventuresome world. The last thing to fall in love with is a particular security. It is, after all, just a sheet of paper indicating a part ownership in a corporation. Its use is purely mercenary.

I learned early in my career to be skeptical and flexible, not stubborn, about a stock. I also learned to take quick, small losses rather than to get emotionally involved in a stock that was dragging me down. When I am wrong about a security, I try to take my loss at the 10 percent level.

Some people have been extremely fortunate in the past by falling in love with something that went their way. That is not necessarily proof it will always be that way.

In other words, it's all right to be in love with a security—until it gets overvalued. Then let somebody else fall in love.

8. DIVERSIFY, BUT DON'T HEDGE ALONE

Hedging—going long on some stocks and short on others—saved most of my resources in 1929, but I do not recommend it. You could *lose* your resources trying it. You run a big risk of losing on both the long and the short. Hedging is a very difficult procedure, unless you find an exact hedge, which doesn't happen very often.

Hedging has permitted me to have an anchor to windward. It has given me more patience to hold on to undervalued long positions. And it has made me less concerned about the psychology of fear that dominates the market from time to time.

I personally hedge because I had such a good experience with it after I developed my own system of hedging. When I went short on Radio Corporation in 1929 and remained long on the rest of my portfolio, it didn't make any difference to me which way the market went. If it went up, I would make money on one set of securities; if it went down, I could hold my own on the other set. My hedging proved to be a timely and profitable move. The bear market that occurred in 1930 to 1932 made it imperative to sell short if you wanted to make a profit. The habit has become somewhat ingrained in me by now, though it is quite possible to do well without it.

Professionals in the commodities markets use hedging for protection. Sometimes newcomers to the market use hedging as a way of gambling. I don't approve of this, but there is no law against it.

Hedge funds are really a modern form of *arbitrage*: A century ago, when you bought the same security in New York and London, there was just a little variation in price from one city to the other. The professional bought the identical security in one city and sold it in another for a very small, but almost sure, profit.

Both the gain factor and the risk factor were far less than in today's *risk arbitrage*, which, believe me, is *very* risky.

Although I hedge for my own account, it is not possible for the amateur investor to do it alone. Hedging carries no guarantees of any kind. It requires a lot of discipline, and you can lose money on either side or on both sides.

If you insist on hedging and have experienced help in doing it, be sure that it is accompanied by reasonable diversification. Be comprehensive in your outlook:

Make sure that some of your principal is kept safe, try to increase your income as well as your capital, and *diversify your investments.*

Since 1929, I have had no losing years, though there were a few years in which I merely broke even. In those years, I still learned a lot. And then some years have been phenomenal. Diversification has been an important part of the winning formula. Don't take my word for it. Read Gerald Loeb, who wrote a great deal on the subject of putting all your eggs in one basket. At one time, many years ago, he put all his eggs in the New York Central and the Pennsylvania railroads. They both went bankrupt.

You should know that only a small portion of the population has all of its money in the market. Investors range from those with less than 10 percent of their wealth invested in securities to those with 100 percent. When interest rates are very high, the average person should consider putting a considerable portion of one's position in bonds.

To achieve balance, one must be flexible. I know an investor who bought his first bond after 50 years of doing very well without bonds. He was flexible enough to realize that after half a century, the time had come.

9. WATCH THE ENVIRONMENT

By *environment* I mean the general market trends as well as the world outside the market. In adapting any of the formulas I have suggested, you need to adapt them to the current market in which you are operating.

In assessing general market conditions, *look at*

percents more than amounts. A drop of 100 points is significant, but it may be less than 2 percent of the market.

Watch energy supplies. Crises in the Middle East have raised the price of crude oil. Oil stocks got overpriced in 1980, leading to a tremendous bear market in oil securities for several years. They went down to one-third or worse.

Watch the sales of American cars. They are becoming much more competitive. In technology, there are a hundred companies to watch. But in the automotive business, there are only three: General Motors, Ford, and Chrysler. General Motors (GM) was poorly managed years ago, but now it is very well managed. It does the greatest gross business of the three, more than $150 billion, and its product has been improved enormously in the past 10 years.

Labor costs in the United States are high compared to the rest of the world. But in China, where the wages are low, they are not yet competing with us in making Boeing (another great company) jets or GM cars.

Ford is not quite as big as GM, but it is equally well managed, with a lot of good products. Chrysler is somewhat smaller than Ford, but it also is better managed than it was in the past.

Economic conditions sometimes play an important role in the market. I have seen precipitous drops stemming from changes in the bond market that were due to increases in business activity as evidenced by the number of people employed. At other times the market pays no attention to economic conditions. For instance, in 1961 the market was highly speculative, especially in new issues. These IPO (initial public offerings) were at too high a price. By 1962 the market had gone down by 35 to 40 percent. But the reason was not economic conditions, which were very good then. The market went down because of internal market conditions.

Don't be overly attentive to the statements of economists. I admire many economists. Many have been my friends and clients. And I have studied economics a great deal, but not to help me in the market. My experience is that the "dismal science" is not worth a damn as far as the market is concerned.

Watching the market, I can usually spot the beginnings of recessions and the recoveries from recessions, which often give an investor the chance to recover through so-called conservative investments like Treasury bills, Treasury bonds, and notes. Treasury bills are very often used by big investors. Your money is safer there than in any other place, better than under a pillow.

You don't need an economist to tell you to *watch interest rates*. No single tool is more important for predicting market trends than the trend of interest rates. Low interest, more than anything else, shows that business conditions are poor.

Watch the difference in yield between stocks and bonds. When bond interest remained low in the 1950s, public utility stocks were comparatively very attractive. Later, high yielding bonds began to compete with equities for investment money.

Usually, when both short-term and long-term rates start rising, they tell the stock investor one story: Run for the hills.

Should you watch the weather in making investment decisions? A lot of people do. Mark Twain said: "October is one of the peculiarly dangerous months to speculate in stocks. The others are July, January, September, April, November, May, March, June, December, August, and February."

Are there stocks for the seasons? Should toy stocks be bought in late summer in anticipation of Christmas? Should retail stores in general also be bought then? If you anticipate a hot summer, should beer stocks be bought in the spring?

Even with their infinite minor variations one year to the next, the seasons are really repetitive milestones. Some people, noting that stock market behavior is often repetitive, try to find some correlation to the seasons. Many assume or hope the market will be dull in summer so that vacations can be carefree. But in some years, summer is the time to be around, as witness the price freeze in 1970 and the peak market in the summer of 1929.

In autumn there is often the expectation of an increase in business activity. But sometimes the surprises are hurricanes, also an autumn phenomenon. Then comes bleak winter and everyone thinks the world is cold. Yet there is the hope of the New Year. A bad (icy and cold) winter means more salt and fuel are used. And a snowy winter may mean more skiing and resort business.

Our greatest hopes are in springtime. The birds are on the wing, fresh rainfall and new plants herald daylight saving time, and the world is new again. On Wall Street it's time to judge agricultural developments. Will the world need new fertilizer? Tractors? Hybrid seed? In reality such decisions can be made at any time.

I prefer a stock for all seasons. It's not necessary to invest by the calendar. Just realize that there are opportunities at all times for the adventuresome investor and that the joys of living and investing are enhanced by the variability of the seasons.

10. DON'T FOLLOW THE RULES

At least not slavishly. My views change as economic, political, and technological changes occur on our planet and sometimes out in space. It is imperative that you be willing to change your thoughts to meet new conditions.

Don't do exactly what I do. If you do, you will go crazy. You have to dig for yourself, just as I do. Wall Street is a wonderful, exciting game. It is invigorating for me to use my brain to analyze what is going on. If I have taught you how to use your brain in a different way, then I will have fulfilled the first mission of a teacher—to make oneself expendable. And you will have learned the most important lesson—*how* to learn.

More than 90 percent of all investors are bulls. A very small percentage are bears. It is not easy to be a bear because it goes against the grain of optimistic Americans who don't like to feel that the world is going to end tomorrow. I don't like to feel that way either. But I always know that it will *change* tomorrow.

The bear market is where I do well because I am an optimistic contrarian. If a lot of people become pessimistic, I become bullish, and vice versa. At the same time, I am a hedger, on both sides of the market.

I do not urge you to be a bear and certainly not a

hedger. Be from Missouri, the "Show Me" state, and use the same skepticism toward me that I caution you to use toward the market.

I have attempted to show you how I succeeded on Wall Street. You will succeed in your own way. My techniques have changed from time to time as I learned from events and from mistakes. Anyone can make a mistake—the important thing is to recognize an error in judgment as quickly as possible and do something about it.

During 68 years on Wall Street, I have been wrong about 30 percent of the time. That means a lot of losses. But it's the 70 percent right that matters. If any investor had been right all of the time, he or she would have accumulated a considerable portion of the world's wealth. But as you might suspect, always-right investors don't exist, except among liars.

Chapter 12

REFLECTIONS
AT AGE 94

Because I am still working at age 94, people ask me about the future. I know quite a bit about what has already happened, which gives me some ideas about what might lie ahead, but I don't pretend to be a fortune-teller. Knowledge of the past may give us some clues to the future, but the beliefs and actions of new generations will determine it.

WHAT THE FUTURE MAY HOLD

Will there be another panic on Wall Street? Possibly. But safeguards now built into the stock market should protect us from the calamity that befell the United States and the world in 1929 and the ensuing years.

A lot depends on whether the wealthiest people in the United States understand that they really do not need to become ever so much wealthier. They already have enough money, and most of them, I believe, give too little to charity and to vital government programs.

There have been 26 bear markets already in this century. History certainly leads one to believe in the inevitability of a 27th. No one can divine how long it will last or where it will go.

Wendell Willkie, the anti-isolationist Republican who ran for President in 1940 and later traveled abroad as President Roosevelt's special representative, wrote a prophetic book, *One World*, in which he predicted the kind of global interdependence that we now assume. It is safe to predict that the world will keep on shrinking.

World domination shifts from one country to another. In the 19th century, Alexis de Tocqueville predicted that the United States and Russia would dominate the 20th century. It turned out he was right. If I were to take a guess about the 21st century, I would suggest that it will be dominated by Asia, led not by Japan but by China, which already has a population of more than 1 billion. The Chinese are a great people of high intellect; they are extraordinarily resourceful, inventive, and ambitious. After all, they invented the wheel—a simple thing, but crucial to the history of humankind.

The United States is bound to remain important in the 21st century because it, too, is an inventive country, with an increasingly strong service economy. Our culture is more diversified than China's. We have in our country many more Asians than China has Americans or Europeans.

I can't predict all the economic and geopolitical implications, but, clearly, the growth of China as a world power will be central to the future of Wall Street and of the American economy and foreign policy.

It should be of no small concern that Americans know so little about China and that Washington has so few experts to focus policy in that area. This dangerous situation is in part, I believe, a lingering outgrowth of the McCarthy era, when the character and effectiveness of many China experts were destroyed.

THE NEUBERGER FOUNDATION

Part of my philosophy is that if you make money, you should spend it, and spend it on something that is important to you.

In 1995 I wanted to increase my annual contribution to the Ethical Culture Society and encourage others to give more; so I gave a challenge grant, seeking matching funds. The grant was made by the Neuberger Foundation, which was established in 1954 to serve as a conduit for some few hundred separate charitable gifts each year. (I get a daily update on the status of the foundation. I don't know why they give it to me so often. Maybe that's something you have to put up with in the computer age.)

In addition to the Society and the Ethical Culture schools, a substantial number of other nonprofit institutions receive grants from the Neuberger Foundation, including art organizations. I have given to the American Federation of Art for half a century. But I have never bought a work of art through the foundation—all the art I own was purchased with my own money.

One of my greatest pleasures has come from gifts to the Metropolitan Museum of Art. I have also given enthusiastically to the Museum of Modern Art from its early days. I believe it has become the greatest museum of its kind in the world.

The Foundation makes it possible for me to tender a $5 million challenge grant to the Purchase College Foundation, on the campus where the Neuberger Museum of Art is located. I am challenging the people of Westchester and nearby Fairfield County in Connecticut to match the grant, over a period of three to five years, for the benefit of the museum and the entire Purchase College campus.

I am suggesting that my daughter Ann be the next head of the Foundation. Originally, it wasn't a family foundation, but I decided a few years ago that I wanted to bring my children into it. Up to this point, I have made the decisions about where to give. Sometimes my family has made valuable suggestions. In passing on the Foundation to future generations, I am aware of the lessons that my children can learn and the pleasure they will derive from giving as they gain deeper understanding of the Emersonian idea that the donor is in fact the recipient.

I have especially enjoyed making gifts in honor of my wife, among them contributions over the years to Bryn Mawr College, her alma mater, which she served as a trustee. Recently, in Marie's honor, I made a challenge grant to the Women's City Club, an influential activist group whose studies of urban problems and recommendations for reform have often helped mold public policy. Marie served several terms as president of the group and was active for many years.

We also lend our support to public television and to hospitals, particularly Lenox Hill Hospital.

Having lived next to Central Park most of my life, I make an annual donation to the Central Park Conservatory, which I think does a very fine job helping to preserve a uniquely beautiful jewel. Several million people use Central Park over the spring, summer, and fall weekends. Even on weekdays there are always plenty of people enjoying the park.

As an individual I believe in giving to individuals in need. I can't do that through the Foundation; but lately, giving as one individual to another, I have found that there are a great many in need. Helping them is truly gratifying.

Those of us who are fortunate enough to have achieved financial success have a high responsibility to our children, to our nation, and to our community.

It is heartening to learn of philanthropists who carry out that responsibility without fanfare or plaques on buildings. In January 1997, I read about just such a man, Charles Feeney, whom I admire tremendously. He has distributed more than $600 million to centers of education and culture in complete anonymity.

I have never met Charles Feeney nor would I know about his generosity had he not been forced by law to disclose the existence of his foundations after many years of philanthropic activity. I salute Mr. Feeney for his humility, his strong sense of purpose, and his devotion to the quality of our society.

EXERCISE AND LONGEVITY

Sometimes I am asked about my longevity. What did I do to reach 94? I engage in an endangered activity that has almost been eradicated by the automobile. It is called walking.

Of course, there are other ingredients in my contest with Father Time. Luck is a big one. Happiness helps. So does moderation in all things. And don't forget—especially if you are retired—to keep busy with some kind of work that exercises the mind.

My father, whom I knew for only 12 years, often recited to me Ben Franklin's advice: Early to bed and early to rise/ Makes a man healthy, wealthy and wise.

It made good sense then and it makes good sense now. I get up between 5:30 and 6:00 in the morning, immediately do a modest amount of exercise, and then jump into the shower.

I turn on CNN to catch up on the overnight news,

have breakfast at 7 o'clock and try to read three newspapers, which is impossible: the *New York Times*, the *Wall Street Journal*, and *Investor's Business Daily*. The latter two I take with me to the office. Usually I leave the *Times* home for later, except for the Tuesday Science section, which I give to Jimmy McCloud, my driver. He knows a lot about science.

Sometime between 7:50 and 8 o'clock—8 at the latest—I meet my friends for a walk in Central Park, where there is less wind than on Fifth Avenue. The wind is even worse on Riverside Drive, but Fifth Avenue is a wind-swept canyon. I find that New York has a lot of wind lately, and not just from the politicians. Of course, I am not as good a walker as I used to be. When I was 80, I could walk very long distances.

Over the years I have walked with a number of different people. Currently, it is with Al Fineman, an investment counselor, and Abe Kanner, whose wife died in 1996. Abe is an old friend and a lovely man, a true intellectual who is also a successful businessman. The three of us walk until 8:30 or so and then go to our respective offices.

By 8:45 in the morning, I have exercised, read the newspapers, eaten breakfast, watched some television news, walked for 30 or 40 minutes, arrived at the office, turned on the computer, and faced the day.

Three times a week—Monday, Wednesday, and Friday—I work out with a personal trainer from 5:00 to 5:45 P.M. In 45 minutes I do 42 exercises. (Some take longer than a minute, some less.) It costs $45, so it is a dollar a minute—well worth it. They are simple exercises that anyone can do, for example:

1. Lean against a chair. Raise one leg, knee bent. Kick out. Repeat 10 times on each leg.
2. Get up and down from your chair 20 times.
3. Lie on the couch and pull your knees up to your chest 24 times.
4. Do easy weight lifting with 5-pound and 3-pound weights.

These and the other 38 exercises can be done standing up, lying in bed, or sitting in a chair.

I work hard especially to improve the strength of my legs so that I can walk a little faster and a little further.

ETHICAL CULTURE

Money makes the world go 'round, but I don't believe in it. I know that art doesn't make the world go 'round, but I do believe in it.

If that sounds paradoxical, don't worry about it. Long ago I found a group of people with whom I am philosophically comfortable. The Ethical Culture Society has proved to be a guiding factor in my life and a central force, both socially and educationally, in Marie's and my life together. My wife's family first introduced me to Ethical Culture. I have always been grateful to the Salant family for that introduction to the Society, where I remain an active member to this day. I served for four years as president and also helped form a Friends committee to lend financial support. Marie and her brothers were graduates of the superb Ethical Culture Schools: the Ethical Culture School for young children (the largest and, in my opinion, the best private grade school in New York City) and Fieldston, the renowned secondary school in the Riverdale section of the city. Later in life, Marie was chairperson of the Ethical Culture Schools for 13 years.

Our three children also graduated from those schools. They received wonderful educations and were inspired by Dr. Algernon Black, the leader of the Society for many years, who taught an ethics class for children.

The founder of Ethical Culture, Felix Adler, was succeeded as leader by another extraordinary man, John Lovejoy Eliot, whom I have good reason to remember well. He officiated at Marie's and my wedding on June 29, 1932. Ethical Culture is a quasi-religion, a philosophy of life that had tremendous appeal to me then and still does. It stresses the importance of education, of knowledge about others, and of leading an ethical life: dealing with all people with respect, living by the golden rule to treat others as you would have them treat you. It urges that we accomplish as much as our abilities permit, in keeping with ethical and moral standards and in service to the community and to humanity.

That credo is not always observed by either side in the Middle East, Bosnia, Northern Ireland, and elsewhere. I worry about big religion because I believe it is the cause of many of our wars in this last decade of the 20th century. Of the big religions, I prefer the Society of Friends, the Quakers.

Ethical Culture calls upon people to do good by

looking at the facts of life rather than the myths. It doesn't believe in influencing people in everything they do, but inspires them to do the best they can. Perhaps its very practicality is one of the reasons that Ethical Culture (legally a religion) has fewer adherents than other religions. It has something positive to offer in the way of attitudes, habits, and character, but it doesn't have the allure of beautiful churches and stained glass windows.

It should be an infinitely larger institution. It deserves to have millions of members, but the whole movement has only thousands. To come to philosophical conclusions through an idealistic, humanistic viewpoint would be good for the world at large. Members of the Society have made important contributions to their communities. Many people are Ethical Culturists without knowing it. Ethical Culture deserves serious investigation by all sensitive individuals who believe that the world can be better and who are willing to participate in making it better.

WHAT GOVERNMENT CAN DO

The American government tends to concentrate on some of the wrong things. It is not paying enough attention to education. Our educational institutions will make our economy grow much more rapidly than will corporate mergers.

President Clinton has shown some recognition of the importance of education in his budget proposals, but government in general seems more interested in policies that enable the rich—the top 2 or 3 percent of the population—to become richer while 20 to 25 percent of the people barely get by.

For all his flaws, Clinton has made real progress toward a balanced budget. Reagan, for all his charming personality, created some of the worst problems with which we struggle now, including the decline of the dollar and the multi-trillion-dollar national debt.

Balancing the budget is very important, but our society has other problems of higher priority. A constitutional amendment requiring a balanced budget would rob the people, the Congress, and the President of their ability to set different priorities at different times in our history during the 21st century.

We need to take a closer look at the defense budget, which grew rapidly in the 1980s at the same time that tax cuts were vastly increasing the debt. The United States cannot afford to be the police force of the entire world. It should, however, pay dues to the United Nations, which brings nations together in support of all kinds of urgent humanitarian projects, many of which are not even in the news.

We should also ensure that enormous sums are not spent for the benefit of the defense contractors while the men and women of the military are poorly paid, many of them training with weapons, vehicles, and aircraft that badly need replacement parts. Thousands of military families are on food stamps. This is a national disgrace.

If we are to reach a balanced budget by the year 2002, I believe that we will need to tax gasoline at least half as high as they do in Europe. We could bring in an extra $100 billion a year, take care of the people who are really hurting, and restore fiscal stability to the government.

That policy would also have the advantage of improving our environment by inhibiting use of the personal car and getting more people into rapid transit. It is unfortunate that the automobile has become so overabundant, not only here, but in other nations. Early in 1996, Thomas Friedman wrote in the *Times* about conditions in Bangkok: he said great things are being done in industry there, but traffic is so bad you can't get around the city.

I propose a tax only half as high as in Europe because most people in the United States have to drive longer distances. If the gas tax is substantially raised, geographical considerations should apply, particularly where there are long distances to commute to work and little or no public transportation. Cutting back on Amtrak is a very short-sighted policy.

Cutting back on the IRS staff is also a great mistake for the country. More people will be able to get away with underpaying their taxes.

Among the programs that could use those lost tax revenues is government support for a scientific effort to harness the sun's energy. Solar power has a simplicity that may appeal more to someone related to art than to scientists. But two decades ago, some cities were already trying it. If it costs too much for private industry to do it, the public interest may need public funds. One important side effect of solving our energy problems with renewable energy sources is that we would not be beholden to oil-rich nations.

We need some straight talk about Social Security. It is ridiculous for people to have their careers ended before they are 75. You wouldn't do that with an artist or a great musician. We would be a far more productive country if we valued the experience, wisdom, and competence of older workers and executives who are often at the peak of their careers when they face mandatory retirement.

It remains to be seen what the Clinton administration and the Republican Congress will do about the health care problem. No country has a health care system that is perfect. If you get free medical service, as they do in some countries, you don't get first-class health care. You can't pick a doctor of your choice. I like to see *my* doctor, not someone selected by the government or by a health maintenance organization (HMO).

We should be concerned about the effect that cost cutting and profit taking by HMOs will have on programs of medical research in the United States. My father lived to the age of 64, which was a little more than average at the time. In the next century, medical advances could increase life expectancy to 120 years. But research toward that end—including a cure for cancer—is expensive and of little interest to most HMOs.

Some progress has been made in recent years on the role of women in government and private enterprise, but we are still far behind on issues of equal responsibility and equal pay. Women have been given short shrift for centuries. It is beyond comprehension that in America in the 20th century women had to fight to win the right to vote. I look forward, in my lifetime, to seeing women play a much larger role in running the United States. A woman could easily be a better president than a man. Eleanor Roosevelt might have been better than Franklin. I don't know much about Mrs. Harding, but anybody would have been better than Warren Harding. There is no question in my mind that we will have a woman president in the first half of the 21st century.

SPOTTING A FUTURE PRESIDENT

It's not easy. At the time of FDR's death in 1945, many people thought of Vice President Harry Truman—if they thought of him at all—as a mediocre, small-town politician with a short fuse. But character emerges in times of challenge.

As it turned out, Harry Truman was a true man in every way. There was no nonsense about him. And he was a learned man, mostly self-educated. I wonder if he would succeed today. He would be impatient with the practice of taking polls before coming to a decision.

On the other hand, John Lindsay, whom I have known quite well, is a wonderful man, handsome and articulate. He looked like a president. But he never went very far in his quest for the presidency.

Lindsay, who was my congressman before he was elected mayor of New York City in 1965, did a number of fine things. He walked the streets of Harlem, made people feel that the city government cared. Lindsay had a charisma that gave New York a psychological lift. But overall, Lindsay was not a good mayor and, therefore, would not have been a good president. He gave too much away. He waged public battles with the unions, which made him appear to be a champion of the public interest. But he lost the battles. In the end the unions got much more from him than they had from his predecessor, Mayor Robert Wagner Jr., who was friendlier with the union leaders.

The so-called moderate wing of the Republican Party has produced some fine candidates. Lindsay, who later switched to the Democratic Party (as I advised Nelson Rockefeller to do), would have been an excellent senator. Wendell Willkie would have been a good president. Rockefeller would have been a great president.

If I had known Nelson before his divorce, I would have said, "Cut out this nonsense. Stay married. You and Happy can carry on your relationship, but don't get divorced." The divorce really damaged him politically, confirming the worst Republican fears that he was too liberal. A divorce used to be considered fatal in politics, particularly with Catholic and conservative voters. John Kennedy, who was as active with the ladies as Rockefeller (if not more so), understood the political necessity of an enduring marriage—especially to a lovely and much admired First Lady. FDR, despite his warm friendships with women, never would have been foolish enough to divorce the great Eleanor Roosevelt.

A whispering campaign in 1952 about Adlai Stevenson's divorce undermined his reputation as an excellent governor of Illinois and a brilliant speaker and writer. People also suspected that he was too much of a soul searcher to be a decisive president, and they may have been right. But I was very impressed by Mr. Stevenson as a person.

Of course, Stevenson never had a chance, running in 1952 and again in 1956 against one of the most popular war heroes in our history, General Dwight Eisenhower. The famous "Ike" smile had been a great reassurance to Americans during World War II, especially as the strain began to show on President Roosevelt's normally cheerful face. "I Like Ike" was a campaign slogan with which the English and other Europeans agreed. But President Eisenhower has always been something of a mystery to me. He was widely popular and yet people never really knew him.

When Senator George McGovern was running for president in 1972, he wanted to meet some Wall Street people. So a reception was held in a West Side hotel, not a ritzy place. I liked McGovern instantly. I thought he was a very decent person and a man of consequence, but not tough enough for the White House.

McGovern was the very opposite of his opponent, Richard Nixon, who was tough, politically brilliant, and a crook. Nixon's toughness was evident very early— in the 1946 smear campaign that won him a seat in Congress and then in his totally unfair senatorial campaign in 1950 against Helen Gahagan Douglas, the highly respected California Congresswoman who was a distinguished actress and the wife of the actor Melvyn Douglas. The Nixon presidency, as we learned from White House tapes, was even more vicious than we knew at the time of the Watergate hearings. The whole thing was predictable from his first campaigns in California.

At the beginning of the primaries in 1992, few predicted that Bill Clinton would be the next president. He seemed to have too many political liabilities. But I liked the Bill Clinton who came before the voters in November 1992 better than the Bill Clinton of November 1996. The first time, as a challenger, he put all the real problems of the country on the table, something not done by his predecessors, Ronald Reagan and George Bush, either as challengers or incumbents.

American voters like to like their presidents. But the voters are more sophisticated than many politicians think. It would appear from the polls that job ratings are based on other factors. Hard as he tries to be loved by everyone, President Clinton is not widely liked. Yet people feel he's doing a good job.

THE ECONOMY RULES THE ELECTION

Most elections hinge in large part on the economic indicators. The economy was beginning to show signs of improvement in November 1992, but it was too late to save President Bush. When Clinton faced the voters as an incumbent four years later, the economy was showing some signs of weakness, but it was still too strong for Senator Bob Dole to go on the attack successfully.

Spotting a future president is as difficult as predicting the economy. The juxtaposition of personalities, events, and trends determines the outcome. All those high-priced political consultants and television and radio commercials make very little difference in the end. Even if Herbert Hoover had saturated the airwaves with commercials in 1932, the Panic of 1929 and its aftermath would have doomed him as a reelectable president and opened the door for the ebullient Franklin Roosevelt.

There is talk of future presidents Al Gore, Jack Kemp, Christine Whitman, Richard Gephardt, Bill Bradley, and a slew of others. But unpredictable events will offer or deny each of them a successful campaign in the year 2000.

THE IMPACT OF WAR

Even more than the economy, war is the great political unknown. When I was 13 years old, Woodrow Wilson was reelected on the slogan "He Kept Us Out of War." But the following year, President Wilson, who had been the peace candidate, responded to public outrage over German submarine warfare by urging America's entry into World War I to "Make the World Safe for Democracy."

Roosevelt, despite his failing health, was elected a fourth time in 1944 on the warning "Don't Change Horses in Midstream," the middle of World War II. The survival of civilization was at stake, not merely the victory or defeat of certain nations. We had no choice but to go all out to win that war.

In the early years of the Cold War, anti-Communist feeling was so strong that Truman was able to come to the aid of South Korea against North Korea in 1950 with little protest. Truman's successor, Eisenhower, got us out of there as fast as he could. He knew that a land war in Asia was bad business. It was too far away for either a good offense or defense. Nearly a half-century later, the hostility between North Korea and South Korea is just as strong and volatile.

My opinion is that nobody really wins a war. Everybody loses a war. The Vietnam War changed America. We lost the war, and we lost some of our character. Our currency was weakened, and our national character was weakened.

Who could have predicted the effect of the Vietnam War on future presidents? One man who saw trouble was the publisher John Knight, one of the earliest and wisest critics of our policy in Vietnam. In 1954 I read a Knight editorial warning us to stay out of the Vietnamese struggle. French President Charles de Gaulle gave us the same advice. I agreed with them. So did my son Roy, who wrote early editorials on the subject.

President Kennedy, a confirmed Cold Warrior, intensified the role of "military advisors" in Vietnam. During the 1961 Vienna summit with Nikita Khruschev, Kennedy told James Reston of the *New York Times* that the Russian premier was showing very little respect for American power in their conversations. The place we would show Khruschev our strength, Kennedy said, would be in Vietnam.

Kennedy's successor, Lyndon Johnson, the peace candidate against Barry Goldwater in 1964, sent in many thousands of troops at the urging of Kennedy's advisors. Richard Nixon, who years before had urged that we send in paratroopers to help the French in Vietnam, was elected in 1968 after convincing many voters that he could achieve "Peace with Honor." He proceeded to escalate the bombing of North Vietnam and to bomb Cambodia as well.

I have always been concerned about the impact of the war in Vietnam on the young people who were sent to fight it and on the families who lost their children. The thousands who were wounded or traumatized, and even those who emerged whole, suffered a terrible disillusionment with the United States. I think the young people who protested were right. Leaders, like Robert McNamara, who insisted that our Vietnam policy was correct, have now admitted they were wrong.

The world is still a tinderbox. Terrible things have been happening in Zaire and Rwanda, in Albania, Nigeria, the Sudan, Bosnia, Tibet, East Timor, Colombia, the Middle East, and many other parts of the globe that will be the focus of tomorrow's news.

What critical events will set the stage for the presidential campaign of 2000?

The 20th century has been one of appalling violence. I hope that our next president, ushering us into a new century, will find a route to peace.

A LITTLE READING GOES A LONG WAY

It's sad to see that so many American households have become increasingly bookless. I have learned more from reading than from formal education. Harry Truman, who I believe will go down in history as one of our most effective national leaders, was perhaps the best-read president we have ever had. I know that because I read a book about him (David McCullough's *Truman*).

Books not only broaden our horizons, they help us make practical choices. I don't mean the how-to manuals. I mean the books from which we gain knowledge—as I did from the biography of Van Gogh—that inspire us to action.

Many people jump from one screen to the other—computer to television and back again—without pausing to read the newspaper, much less a good book. Of course, newspapers are increasingly available on the computer, as books will be, too. But I still like holding the *Wall Street Journal* when I read it. For professional reading, the *Journal* is indisputably my most important tool. I like the *Journal*'s method of putting succinct messages on the front page. If I want to read further into a story, as I often do, I turn to another page.

I read the *New York Times* every day with great pleasure, particularly the financial section. If I am in Europe, I am delighted to get the *Herald Tribune*, a paper that I wish we could still get in New York each morning. It was a welcome supplement to the *Times*.

Other papers I enjoy reading are *The Economist*, one of the world's truly great publications, and the *Investor's Business Daily*, which is at least equal in quality to the *Wall Street Journal*.

But books are the closest to my heart. Many of the milestones of my life are marked by the well-worn books still on a shelf in my office, including a first edition of James Joyce's *Ulysses*. I associate each of those books with a major turning point in my life. Ralph Waldo Emerson's essay *On Compensation* helped me recognize that the person who gives receives even more than the person who receives.

As this memoir comes to an end, I dare to hope that this book will be on someone else's shelf as a helpful signpost along the way.

SO FAR, SO GOOD

Looking back, I realize that in my forties I was handling the Guardian Mutual Fund and my private accounts and I was president of the Ethical Culture Society and of the American Federation of Art, the largest national art organization. I was buying and giving away art, reading voraciously, and enjoying family life, cultural life, and social life.

Today I am just as busy. For me, life is still a great adventure. I am excited by the prospect of each day and by the advent of a new millennium.

When you reach my age, you also learn to live with times of sadness. Most of my oldest friends have passed on, one by one. And on Mother's Day, May 11, 1997, as I was approaching the end of this memoir, my beloved wife Marie died. My memories of Marie as a young woman, and as we grew older together, are vivid and enduring.

Much of this book has necessarily centered on the past. One learns from the past, but when I go to the office in the morning, I am very much in the present and always looking toward the future.

Overall, life has been good to me. I have a wonderful family and an exhilarating career. I hope that by sharing with you, the reader, some of the good times and some of the not-so-wonderful times, I have given you food for thought and encouragement for action in the future. I wish you good health and good luck.

About the Connables

Alfred and Roma Connable, who assisted their friend Roy Neuberger in the preparation of his memoirs, are graduates of the University of Michigan, where they met while working on the college newspaper. They reside on Long Island, New York, and have two sons (Ben, a Marine officer, and Joel, a broadcast journalist in Los Angeles). The Connables have been marriage and writing partners for 35 years.

Index

Aldrich, Lucy, 147
American car sales, impact on
    stock market, 180
American Federation of Art,
    118–123, 189
American Telephone &
    Telegraph (AT&T),
    35, 92, 94–96, 164
Annenberg, Walter,
    Ambassador, 127
Anti-Semitism, 129
Arbitrage, 178
Art, interest in, 15. *See
    also* Art collection,
    artists in collection
Art collection, *see specific
    museums*
  artists in collection, 115
  development of, 107
  donations from, 113–117
Asia House, 148–149
Austin, Darrel, 115
Avery, Milton, 111–115
Avery, Sally, 111, 113
Avnet, Lester and Joan, 136
Avon Products, 100, 176

Balanced funds, 93
B. Altman, employment at,
    3, 12–16, 154
Barr, Alfred, 110, 120
Baruch, Bernard, 172
Baur, Jack, 120
Bear, Joseph Ainslee, 33
Bear, Stearns, 33
Bear market:
  charts of, 168–169
  investors in, 183
  1973–1974, 100
  post-Panic market, 43
  Stock Market Panic of
    1929, 39
Bennett, Mrs., 91
Berman, Robert, 74–76
Beta, defined, 39
Bierstadt, Albert, 124
Bing, Al, 98
Black, Algernon, Dr., 194
Black Tuesday, 38
Bliss, Lily, 109
Blotters, 34
Boating Party, The (Renoir),
    108

Boy from the Plains (Hurd), 109–110
Breeskin, Adelyn, 121
Brooklyn Museum, 115–116
Brown, J. Carter, 121
Browne, Byron, 113
Bruce, Patrick Henry, 135
Buffett, Warren, 96, 158–160
Bull market, 45, 171, 183
Burghers of Calais, The (Rodin), 137

Café des Deux-Magots, 22–24
Career development:
  early years, xi, 3, 12–16, 154
  merchandising, 13–15, 154
  in Paris, 26–27
  Wall Street, *see* Wall Street, career development
Cezanne, 26
Charts, 168
Checkerboard (Avery), 111
Chicago Art Institute, 135
Childhood:
  birth, 3–4
  move to New York, 6–7
Children, birth of, 67–68
Chrysler (Corporation), 180
City Patrol Corps, 73
Clinton administration, 195–196, 198, 201–202
Cloisters, 126
Coca-Cola, 95–96, 157
Cold War, 203–204

Cole, Thomas, 124
Commodities, hedging in, 178
Common Stocks for Long-Term Investment (Smith), 175
Computer technology, impact of, 80–83
Confessions of a Young Man (Moore), 26
Conglomerates, 167
Corcoran Gallery, 108
Courtship, 61–62
Crawford, Ralston, 115
Cullen, Countee, 11
Cunningham, Charlie, 120
Customer broker, 52

Danzig, Jerome, 33
DaVinci, 127
Davis, George, 79
Davis, Stuart, 115
de Groot, Adelaide Milton, 115, 127
de Koonig, Willem, xii
de Montebello, Philippe, 120, 124, 128
Depreciation, 175
de Tocqueville, Alexis, 187
D'Harnoncourt, Rene, 120
Despres, Emile, 83, 97
Dewey, Thomas E., 47
Dillon, Douglas, 128
Diversity, importance of, 177–179
Dividends, company analysis, 174
Divorce, personal thoughts on, 200

Donations, to art
    collections, 114–117
Downtrends, 170
Dudensing, Valentine, 112–
    113
Dumas, Alexandre, 26

Earnings, long-term/short-
    term, 175–176
Economic conditions,
    impact on:
    elections, 202–203
    stock market, 180–181
Eddy, Charles, 72–73
Education:
    art courses, 27
    DeWitt Clinton High
        School, 11
    Kohut School, 8
    New York University:
        economics courses, 82
        School of Journalism, 12
Eilshemius, Louis Michel,
    121, 130
Eisenhower, Dwight, 200–
    201
Elliott, John Lovejoy, 61,
    194
Elsworth, 148
Energy Fund, 102
Energy supplies, impact on
    stock market, 180
Engagement, 63. *See also*
    Marriage
Erie Canal securities, 173
Ethical Culture Society, 98,
    189, 193–195
Europe:
    Berlin, 27–28

Cannes, 25
Paris, 21–24
travel around, generally,
    19–21
Vienna, 28–29
Exercise, longevity and,
    191–193

Fahnestock & Company,
    73–74
F A R Gallery, 24
February Feeding (Maccoy),
    109
Federal Reserve, 82
Feininger, Lyonel, 122
Fels, Floret, 29
Fineman, Al, 192
Flexibility, importance of,
    176–177, 179
FOCUS, 102
Ford (Motor Company), 180
Forsyte Saga (Galsworthy),
    16
Founding Friends of the
        Neuberger Museum,
    142, 146–147
Friedman, Thomas, 197
Friedsam, Michael, 14, 20
Fujita, 26

Gans, Victor, 130
Gaspe Landscape (Avery),
    111–112
Gedeon, Lucinda, 147
GEICO, 159
General Motors, 180
Glickenhaus, Seth, 98
Goldwater, Barry, 139, 204
Goodrich, Lloyd, 120

Goodyear, Conger, 109
Gould, Samuel, 138, 142
Government intervention,
    personal thoughts
    on, 195–199
Graham, Ben, 158–159
Great Depression, 43, 53–54,
    169
Grebstein, Sheldon, 146
Grizzly bear market, 169
Gropper, William, 115
Growth stock, 174
Gruber, Alan, 98
Guardian Mutual Fund:
    beginning of, 88–90
    Board of Directors, 97–99
    common stock and, 93–94
    current status, 90–92, 103
    philosophies of, 92–93
    quantum gains, 94–97
    value investing, 157–158

Hale, Robert Beverly, 123–
    124
Halle, Stanley, 56
Halle & Stieglitz, 33–35, 51,
    55–57
Hart, Kitty Carlisle, 129,
    147–150
Hartley, Marsden, 115
Hawaiian Global
    Environmental Fund,
    101
Health care trends, personal
    thoughts on, 198
Health maintenance
    organizations
    (HMOs), personal
    thoughts on, 198

Hedging, 36–37, 177–179
Herald Tribune, 206
Hine, Cordelia (Detsie), 78
Hine, Donald, 78–79
Hirshhorn, Joseph, 137–138
Hirshhorn Sculpture
    Garden, 137–138
Hofmann, Hans, xii, 124
Holty, Carl, 113
Homer, Winslow, 116
Honeymoon, 64. *See also*
    Marriage
Hoover administration, 53
Hopper, Edward, 142
Houghton, Arthur, 129
Hoving, Thomas, 120, 125–
    128
Hurd, Peter, 109, 115

IBM, 173, 176
Influences on stock market:
    American car sales, 180
    economic conditions,
    180–181
    energy supplies, 180
    interest rates, 181
    weather, 181–182
    yields, 181
Intellectuals (Johnson), 23
Interest rates, 179, 181
International investments,
    155
Intrinsic value, 172
Intuition, importance of, 21,
    170. *See also*
    Timing
Investment strategies:
    future directions, 187–188
    hedging, 36–37, 177–179

long-term, 166–169
selling short, 45, 171
successful, *see* Successful
    investing, ten
    principles of
Investment trusts:
    closed-end, 88, 100–102
    open-end, 88
Investors, discussion:
    in bear and bull markets,
    183
    institutional, 174
    sheep market, 165–166
    small, 102–103, 153
Investor's Business Daily,
    192, 206
IPO (initial public offering),
    180–181
IRS, personal thoughts on,
    197

Japan Fund, 102
Jervis, Herman, 98
Johns, Jasper, 130
Johnson & Johnson, 45, 157
Johnson, Lyndon,
    administration, 204
Johnson, Philip, 141–142,
    150
Jones, Alfred W., 77–78
Jones, Mary, 77
Junk bonds, 164

Kanner, Abe, 192
Kaplan, Abbott, 138, 145–
    146
Kaplan, Jack, 120, 122
Kassen, Michael, 103
Kendall, Don, 146

Kennedy, John F.,
    administration, 203–
    204
Kennedy, Joseph, 34, 36, 56,
    163–164
Klein, Milton, 12, 14
Kohut School, 8
Kootz, Sam, 113, 121
Kreisler, Fritz, 19
Kreuger, Ivan, 48

Lacy, Bill, 146
Lambert, 35
Lawrence, Jacob, 115
Lee, Sherman, 148
Lehman, Bobby, 126
Lend-Lease Act, 72
Lenox Hill Hospital, 190
Levine, Jack, 115
Lieberman, Alexander, 144
Lindsay, John, 149, 199–200
Lipman, Howard, 76–78,
    118
Lipman, Jean, 77
Lipsher, Milton, 77
Listen to the Money Talk
    (Lipman), 77
Literature, influences of:
    "Advice of an Art
    Historian," 27
    Forsyte Saga
    (Galsworthy), 16
    Intellectuals (Johnson), 23
    On Compensation
    (Emerson), 20, 206
    Ulysses (Joyce), 24, 206
    Vincent van Gogh (Fels),
    29, 206
Loeb, Gerald, 179

London Copper
  Development
  Company, 5
Louvre, 19, 126
Luers, Bill, 124
Lynch, Peter, 93, 160

Maccoy, Guy, 109
McCloud, Jimmy, 147, 192
McLaughlin, John, 79
McNamara, Robert, 205
Magazine of Art, 122
Magellan, 93
Margins, defined, 39
Marin, John, 56, 115
Market conditions:
  analysis of, 179–181
  trends in, 170
Marlborough Gallery, 127–
  128
Marriage, 61, 64, 194
Marx, Karl, 23
Massachusetts Investment
  Trust, 87
Meis, Millard, 129
Merchandising, early career
  in, 13–15
Merrill Lynch, 33
Metropolitan Museum of Art:
  donations to, 123–125, 189
  trustee of, 128–129
Milbank, 89–90
Milken, Michael, 164
Miller, Dorothy, 110
Minute Maid, 95–96
Money management:
  career development, 51
  personal, 35–36
Montgomery Ward, 45

Moore, Henry, 142–143
Moran, Thomas, 124
Morgan Guaranty, 97
Morley, Grace McCann, 120
Morris, George L. K., 115, 124
Murray, Arthur and
  Kathryn, 64
Museum of Modern Art
  (MOMA):
  benefactors of, 114–115
  paintings in, 108, 110
Mutual funds:
  balanced, 93
  Guardian, *see* Guardian
    Mutual Fund
  no-load, 89, 153
  origin, 87–88
  T. Rowe Price, 99–100, 158

Nadler, Marcus, 82–83
NASDAQ, 76
National Gallery, 108
Neuberger, Ann, 67, 189
Neuberger, Bertha
    Rothschild:
  death of, 6
  family background, 5
  marriage of, 5
  memories of, 5, 7–8
Neuberger, Jimmy, 68
Neuberger, Leslie:
  birth of, 5–6
  death of, 10
  marriage of, 10
  relationship with, 9–10
Neuberger, Louis:
  children, 4–5
  Connecticut Web and
    Buckle Factory, 5

death of, 8
family background, 4
London Copper
    Development
    Company, 5
marriage of, 4
memories of, 5
Neuberger, Marie Salant:
    children, 67–68
    courtship, 61–62
    death of, 209
    educational background,
        61–62, 65, 190, 194
    engagement, 63
    family background, 64–
        67, 193
    honeymoon, 64
    life with, generally, 3, 96
    marriage, 61, 107, 194
    Women's City Club, 190
Neuberger, Roy S., 6, 68
Neuberger, Ruth:
    birth of, 6
    children of, 67
    death of, 9
    marriage of, 9
    move to New York, 7
    relationship with, 8
Neuberger&Berman:
    Berman, Robert, 74–76
    clearing by, 33
    computer technology and,
        80–82
    development of:
        client list, 73
        opening the office, 73–74
        timing of, 57
        World War II, 71–73
    Guardian Mutual Fund,

    see Guardian
        Mutual Fund
    Partners Fund, 102–103
    portfolio management,
        90–91
    partners, 76–80
    survival of, 81
    value investing, 157
Neuberger Foundation, 81,
    188–191
Neuberger Museum of Art:
    Avery paintings in, 114
    Kitty Carlisle Hart and
        Asia House, 148
    construction of, 141–142
    development of, 135
    donations to, 150
    establishment of, 109
    funding, 146–147
    opening, 142–145
    Rockefeller, Nelson:
        meeting with, 135–137,
            150
        reply to, 138–139
New Deal, impact of, 53–54
New York Times, 192, 206
New York University, 12, 82
Newhouse, Sy, 130
Nifty Fifty, 100
No-load funds, 89, 153
Noguchi, Isamu, 143–144
Northern Pacific Panic of
    1907, 5
Number 8 (Pollock), 111

Oil stocks, 180
O'Keeffe, Georgia, 56
On Compensation
    (Emerson), 20, 206

One World (Willkie), 187
Osterweis, Steve, 97–98

Pach, Walter, 27
Paris:
    arts in, 26–27, 107
    Café des Deux-Magots,
        22–24
    living in, 21–22
Parsons, Betty, 111
Peore, Emmanuel, 97
PepsiCo, 146
Percents, importance of, 180
Perry, Fred, 25
Personal background:
    children, 67–68
    courtship, 61–62
    engagement, 63
    family, 7–10
    honeymoon, 64
    marriage, 61, 64, 194
    move to Westchester, 68
    parents, 4–7
    siblings, 5–6
Personal computers (PC),
    impact of, 81
Philanthropy, 189–191
Phillips, Duncan, 107–109,
    130–131
Phillips, Lloyd and Ethel, 63
Phillips Gallery, 107–108
Picasso, 121, 130
Polaroid, 100
Pollock, Jackson, 111–112,
    122, 144
Portfolio:
    diversification in, 179
    personal:

Radio Corporation of
    America (RCA), 36–
    37, 39–40, 43, 178
    during Stock Market
        Panic of 1929, 35, 40
Postum, 35
Potter, Aaron, 8–9, 20, 52–
    53, 55, 68
Potter, Jesse, 20
Potter, William, 9, 68
Potter and Schnakenberg, 8–
    9
Presidency, personal
    thoughts on, 199–
    203
Publicity Clock Company, 10
Purchase College
    Foundation:
    future directions, 189
    overview, 145–146
Purdy, Harry, 55

Quidors, James, 124

Racing Club de Paris, 23
Radio Corporation of
    America (RCA), 36–
    37, 39–40, 43, 47,
    51, 178
Rattner, Abraham, 115
Reading habits, importance
    of, 205–207. *See
    also* Literature,
    influences of
Reagan, Ronald,
    administration, 196
Reston, James, 204
Risk arbitrage, 178

Robertson, Bryan, 142
Rockefeller, Abby Aldrich, 109
Rockefeller, Blanchette, 148
Rockefeller, David, 136
Rockefeller, Happy, 136, 147–149
Rockefeller, John D., 136, 148–149
Rockefeller, John D., Jr., 54
Rockefeller, Laurance, 136, 148
Rockefeller, Mark, 149
Rockefeller, Mary, 148
Rockefeller, Nelson:
  death of, 145
  donations from, 147
  influence of, 109–110
  Neuberger Museum of
    Art and, 136–142, 144–145
  as politician, 139–141
Rockefeller Foundation, 120
Rogers, Jimmy, 161–162
Roosevelt, Franklin, 53
  administration of, 71–72, 203
Root, Elihu, Senator, 118
Rorimer, James, 120, 123–125
Rose, Charlie, 148
Rosenberg, Paul, 112–113
Rosenthal, Alan, 91, 96
Rosenthal, Lenore, 96
Rousseau, Henri, 127–128

Salant, Aaron, 61–62, 64–66
Salant, Bill, 62, 66–67, 83
Salant, Dorothy, 67

Salant, Gabe, 65
Salant, Josephine, 64, 66
Salant, Marie. *See*
  Neuberger, Marie
  Salant
Salant, Walter, 62, 66
Salant & Salant, 65–66
Samuel, Donald, 102
Samuelson, Paul, 170
Schapiro, Meyer, 23–25, 99
Schapiro, Morris, 99
Scheider, Alfred, 66
Schenck, Ed, 120
Security Analysis (Graham), 158
Seligman, 88, 159
Selling short, 45, 171
Shahn, Ben, 115
Sheep Market, 165–166
Short-term earnings, 167
Side Fund, 102–103
Simon, Charles, 79, 135
Smith, Edgar, 175
Smythe, Craig, 129
Soby, James, 120
Social Security, personal
  thoughts on, 197–198
Solar power, personal
  thoughts on, 197
Sorbonne, 27
Soros, George, 158, 160–161
Standard & Poor's 500, 156
Standard Oil, 54, 110
State University of New
  York at Purchase,
  137–139, 142. *See
  also* Purchase
  College Foundation

Steinhardt, Michael, 162–163
Stieglitz, Alfred, 56
Stieglitz, Stanley, 56
Stock, generally:
  common, 93–94, 172
  earnings, 175–176
  growth, 174
  price movement, 174–175
  purchase criteria, 167
  yield, 181
Stock Exchange seat, 73, 75
Stock market:
  Crash of 1987, 43–44
  Panic of 1929:
    Crash of 1987 vs., 43–44
    description of, 35, 37–40
    lessons from, 44–46, 169
    suicide and, 48
Straus, Philip, 90–91, 98–99
Strauss, Jerry, 63
Successful investing, ten
    principles of:
  analyze the companies
    closely, 173–176
  beware of the sheep
    market, 165–166
  diversify, but don't hedge
    alone, 177–179
  don't fall in love, 176–177
  don't follow the rules,
    183–184
  get in and out on time,
    170–173
  know thyself, 154–156
  long-term perspective,
    166–169

study the great investors:
  Buffett, Warren, 158–160
  Graham, Ben, 158–159
  Kennedy, Joseph, 163–164
  Lynch, Peter, 160
  Milken, Michael, 164
  Rogers, Jimmy, 161–162
  Soros, George, 158, 160–161
  Steinhardt, Michael, 162–163
  Wilson, Robert, 163
  watch the environment, 179–183
Sullivan, Cornelius, Mrs., 109
Sunset (Avery), 116
Sutton, Willie, 30

Tamayo, Rufino, 115
Taylor, Francis Henry, 120
10 percent rule, 46–48, 171
Tennis:
  city champions, 11
  Cannes circuit, 25
Timing, significance of, 170–173
Trading, historical
    perspective:
  in 1930s, 54
  Stock Market Panic of
    1929, *see* Stock
    market, Panic of
    1929

Treasury bills, 181
Treasury bonds, 181
Treasury notes, 181
Tri-Continental, 88, 101, 159
Trilling, Lionel, 11
T. Rowe Price, 99–100, 158
Truman, Harry,
    administration, 203
Tsai, Gerry, vii

Ulysses (Joyce), 24, 206
Union Pacific, 35
Uprising, The (Daumier), 108
Uptrends, 170
Urf, Armand, 95
Utrillo, 26

Value investing, 157–158
van Gogh, Vincent, 29–30,
    127–128
Velazquez, 127
Vermeers, 119
Vietnam War, 203–204
Vincent van Gogh (Fels), 29,
    205

Walker, Hudson, 121
Walker, John, 121
Wall Street, career
    development
  as customer broker
    client list, 55
    role of, 51–52
  Halle & Stieglitz, 33–35,
    51, 55–57
Wall Street Journal, 192,
    206

War, effects of, 203–205
Washburn, Joan, 135
Washington, Anne, 15
Weather conditions, impact
    on stock market,
    181–182
Weber, Max, 115
Wechsler, Herman, 24
Westchester, residence in,
    68
Whitney, Gertrude
    Vanderbilt, 117
Whitney, Jock, 140
Whitney, Richard, 46–48,
    171
Whitney Museum of
    American Art, 108,
    117–118
Wilder, Thornton, 26
Wills, Helen, 25
Wilson, Robert, 163
Wilson, Woodrow,
    administration, 9–
    10, 203
W & J Sloane, 13
Women's City Club, 190
World War II, 71–73, 169
Wormser, Sam, 79
Wyeth, Andrew, 109

Xerox, 172

Yates, Dr., 55
Yields, 181
Young Artist (Avery), 112

Zicklin, Larry, 80